BYZANTIUM
AND
EUROPE

BYZANTIUM AND EUROPE

SPEROS VRYONIS, JR.

HARCOURT, BRACE & WORLD, INC.

First American Edition 1967

Library of Congress Catalog Card Number: 67-11706

PRINTED IN GREAT BRITAIN BY JARROLD AND SONS LTD NORWICH

BYZANTIUM AND EUROPE

Errata Sheet

Page 51, Plate 31:   For imperial palaces read city

Page 66, Plate 44:   For icon-worshippers read the adherents of the icons

Page 67, Plate 45:   For Leo III read Leo IV; delete was the only woman who

Page 72, Plate 46:   For twelfth-century read fourteenth-century

Page 77, Plate 51:   Delete last of the Macedonian dynasty

Pages 89 and 202, Plate 57:   The Phocas being discussed here is Nicephorus I
  Phocas (963-69), not the earlier Phocas (602-10).

Page 102, Plates 69 and 70:   For monastic life read religious life

Page 116, Plate 79:   For secular art read religious art

Page 140, Plate 93:   For 1104 read 1097

Page 172, Plate 111, 112:   For fourteenth-century read thirteenth-century

Page 184, Plate 121:   Delete The new humanistic approach is seen in this

Page 202, Plate 56:   Delete Leo VI receiving the investiture of Holy Wisdom

Page 203, Plate 59:   Delete Epiphany of

Page 203, Plate 77:   For c. 955 read c. 960

Page 203, Plate 81:   For c. 950 read tenth century

Page 203, Plate 83:   For 969-76 read 1057-59

Page 204, Plates 85 and 88:   For Thirteenth to fourteenth centuries read
  Fourteenth century

Page 204, Plate 98:   For 1130 read 1125

Page 204, Plate 104:   Delete Ms. Gr. 9081. f. 99v.

Page 204, Plate 106:   Delete Probably Hellenistic

Page 204, Plate 114:   For Morae read Morea

Page 205, Plate 121:   For Portrait read Representation

CONTENTS

THE EMPERORS
OF BYZANTIUM

1 Stone portrait of the emperor Diocletian

I TRANSITION FROM ANTIQUITY AND THE EMERGENCE OF BYZANTIUM

The Byzantine empire was born of the third-century crises which transformed the world of antiquity, and though the elements of continuity between the Byzantine world and the world of antiquity are clear and undeniable, so too are the differences. During the course of this momentous transformation the empire lost its Latin-pagan appearance and gradually assumed a Greek-Christian form, though to be sure Byzantium, like the Roman empire, remained a polyglot, multi-national and polysectarian state during the greater part of its existence. The difficulties which the Roman empire experienced in the third century were largely the result of imperfections in the empire's political, social and cultural institutions. It was these innate flaws, rather than the power of the barbarian nations, which prostrated the state and threatened to destroy it in the half-century which preceded the reign of Diocletian. Perhaps the single most serious defect in the whole system was the lack of a regularized imperial succession. By the third century the oft-repeated phrase 'succession by successful revolution', came to describe only too truly the established pattern in the accession to the throne of the Caesars. Dynastic sentiment had failed to take root, and the emasculated senate was usually, though not always, powerless, so that the armies became the ultimate arbiters in the promotion and removal of emperors. Ambitious generals and rapacious troops combined to produce a period of short reigns and violent successions. In the half-century preceding the reign of the great reformer Diocletian there were about twenty rulers (most of whom died violent deaths) with an average reign of two and a half years. This situation had a highly deleterious effect. In so vast an empire the degradation of the ruler to the status of a tool of the armies and the accompanying perversion of the military function were disasters of great magnitude. For the individual around whom the whole system revolved was divested of all respect and authority, and the armies were consumed in selfish enterprises at the expense of the defence of the frontier.

The lack of political stability undoubtedly further aggravated an economic malaise which beset the empire throughout the third century. The causes of this were far more complex than in the case of the political disturbances. The economic ills of the empire included such factors as an unfavourable balance of trade with the Orient, decreasing returns from taxation and disturbance of economic life by the increased civil strife and barbarian raids, the high incidence of the plague and depopulation, increase in the donations paid to the troops and rising administrative expenses. Government had recourse to debasement of the coinage whereby gold money virtually disappeared and silver coin was transmuted into copper money. This debasement induced a meteoric inflation with the result that society began to rely increasingly on a barter economy.

A profound transformation in the moral and spiritual life of the empire was also clearly apparent. The religions of the Greeks and Romans had exhibited their greatest vitality when the *polis* or *civitas* was still the focal point of men's thoughts and actions. But even then the character of Graeco-Roman paganism had been more patriotic than ethical and spiritual. By the third century, at a time when municipal patriotism had been deprived of any substantial basis, Graeco-Roman paganism was largely an historical fossil which promised the individual little. The Oriental mystery cults, combining that mystery, pomp, and ceremony which so appeal to man's emotional character, contrasted sharply with the prosaic indifference of much of Graeco-Roman paganism to man's needs. The appeal of the eastern religions was not exclusively emotional because they also provided a rationale for living the ethical life in this world. Thus if a man shared in the cult of a particular deity and lived according to proper ethical precepts, he was assured of the reward of immortality in the afterlife. This offered further comfort to men at a time when society was coming apart at the seams, and rapacity was often as characteristic of government officials as of bandits and pillaging barbarians.

It has been plausibly supposed that the religions of the East became such formidable competitors to classical paganism not only because of their greater emotional and ethical appeal, but also because the cults had a superior intellectual level. With the rise of philosophy in the Greek world, knowledge had become the special preserve of the philosopher, and was divorced from religion. In the East, where the priestly classes remained a repository of both secular and religious knowledge, there was not this sharp separation between religion and knowledge. Even though it is true that philosophers did increasingly concern themselves with questions of religion, they did so on such an elevated plain that it remained beyond the comprehension of the masses.

Whatever the reasons, there is no doubt that by the third century the trickle of the Nile and the Euphrates into the Tiber had become a torrential flood, and the sects of Mithra, Christ, Cybele, the Jews, Isis and Osiris had spread throughout the empire. This dispersion or dissemination not only acted as a powerful catalyst in the religious and ethical domains, but was to have a profound effect on the political and artistic forms of the succeeding centuries. The revolution which the spread of the Oriental mystery religions effected in the world of the third century, has not attracted the attention its significance warrants. The triumph of Christianity in the fourth century obscured the importance of the third-century phenomenon in the eyes of Christian intellectuals, who were prejudiced against Christianity's competitors.

In modern times, though scholars have appreciated the orientalization of Graeco-Roman paganism, laymen are much more familiar with the barbarian invasion from the north than with the religious invasion from the east. The barbarian penetration of the imperial borders was accompanied by wars, destruction and death, so that the phenomenon was then, and is now, more readily perceptible. Oriental religions triumphed in thousands of insignificant daily encounters, seldom accompanied by any spectacular acts. It is only at the end of this cumulative process that the effect was visible, and by then it had become such an integral part of society that it was taken for granted.

The internal disorganization of the empire greatly facilitated the onslaught of foreign peoples on the empire's northern and eastern frontiers. In Europe the imperial defences along the Rhine and Danube were increasingly penetrated by the Germanic tribes. Beginning on a small scale in the reign of Alexander Severus, these raids attained major proportions by the middle of the century. Saxon pirates rendered the English Channel unsafe, while in 256 the Franks crossed the Lower Rhine, and in slightly more than a decade imperial troops were battling the raiders in both Gaul and Spain. The Alemanni crossed the Rhine in the south and reached as far as northern Italy before being halted. The most powerful of the Germanic tribes seem to have been those of the Goths who in 251 killed the emperor Decius and inflicted the most serious Germanic defeat upon the imperial troops since Varus' legions had been destroyed in the reign of Augustus. Emboldened by their spectacular successes, the Goths not only extended their depredations to the heart of the Balkans (their allies, the Heruli, appeared before Athens in 269), but, taking to the sea, raided the coasts of the Marmara, Black, and Aegean Seas. Claudius Gothicus temporarily halted these attacks south of the Danube, but Aurelian withdrew the last Roman legion from Dacia in 270 and the Goths occupied it unhindered.

In the east the danger did not appear in the form of a new people, as it had in Europe, but in the form of a new dynasty. The Parthian state, which had arisen at the expense of the Hellenistic kingdom of the Seleucids, had by the early third century degenerated into a loosely-held congeries of vassal states. In the southern district of Persia arose a family of fire priests who successfully rebelled against the Arsacids and in 224–26 defeated the last Parthian ruler, Artabanus V, and destroyed the Parthian state. In 226 Ardashir, of the family of Sassan, was crowned shahanshah and a new era in the history of the Near East began, for the emergence of the Sassanids represented more than a mere change of dynasty. This neo-Achemenid state, which soon absorbed the former lands of the Arsacids, was a more centralized and powerful state than that of the Parthians – a fact which the Romans did not in the beginning appreciate. This new monarchy represents the first stage in the process by which the

2 This fourth-century cameo shows the capture of the emperor Valerian by the Sassanid ruler, Shapur I, in 260

Iranian people rejected the last vestiges of Hellenism. The establishment of Zoroastrianism as the official religion of the state, the appearance of a highly-developed hierarchical religious structure with a *mobadhan mobad* (a sort of Zoroastrian pope) at the apex and the establishment of a canonical text of the Avesta, were factors which gave the Sassanid theocratic state an external similarity to Byzantium. The highly stratified social structure with its rigid caste system, however, was immobilized to an extent far beyond anything Diocletian (the son of a freedman) could have conceived.

The first Sassanid rulers regarded themselves as heirs of the last Darius and desired to bring about a re-birth of the Oriental empire which Alexander and his generals had overthrown. Sassanid and Roman (and later Byzantine) armies soon clashed in the border regions of the upper Tigris and Euphrates, Syria, and Armenia. The significance of the change in dynasties became clear in 260 when Shapur I defeated the Roman armies and captured the emperor Valerian. The unexpected but timely appearance of Odenathus of

15

Palmyra and his queen Zenobia halted any further Sassanid conquests and the empire enjoyed a certain respite. Palmyra, as a traditional caravan city living from the proceeds of itinerant commerce and merchants, had become a blooming commercial centre of the typical oasis type, and its prosperity was evident in the thin veneer of Graeco-Roman culture assumed by its Arab inhabitants. By 264 the Arabs of Palmyra had defeated the Persians, restored the boundaries of the Roman empire and acquired the temporary gratitude of Rome.

Though the eastern and northern boundaries of the empire had been restored by the latter half of the century (with the exception of the withdrawal from Dacia), the pressures of Germans and Persians remained constant, awaiting the opportunity which the weakness of the empire would present in the late fourth and fifth centuries.

REFORMS OF DIOCLETIAN AND CONSTANTINE

It was indeed fortunate for the empire that two rulers of unquestionable ability assumed direction of affairs in these critical times. Diocletian (284–305), pre-eminent as an administrator rather than a soldier, had made his way in the Roman *cursus honorum* from the bottom to the very top of the official hierarchy. During these years in the imperial administration he had had ample opportunity to witness the evils besetting the state, and came to the throne rich in that experience so necessary to successful reformers. His successor Constantine, though he rose by violent means, also concerned himself with reform and his reign was in many ways complementary to that of Diocletian. The half-century of reform associated with the reigns of these two monarchs does not represent a sudden departure from the general development of the third century, for the immediate predecessors of Diocletian had already begun the task of taming the administrative, economic, and political chaos, and had attained some modest successes. But it was Diocletian and Constantine who realized the significance of the trend and brought to a successful conclusion this process of change by institutional reform on a large scale. Their measures were not promulgated and put into effect

3 Marble head of Constantine, the first Christian emperor and founder of Constantinople ▶

throughout the empire at a given moment, but rather took shape in a piecemeal fashion during the five and a half decades which separated the accession of Diocletian and the death of Constantine.

It had become obvious to Diocletian that his great empire, so beset by internal problems and foreign attacks, could no longer be effectively wielded by a single ruler with the administrative means employed until then. He therefore created the institution of the tetrarchy in the hope that two augusti and two caesars would succeed where one augustus had failed. In 286 he appointed Maximian augustus in the west, and in 293, when he elevated Constantius and Galerius as caesars in the west and east, the tetrarchic reform was completed. This institutional advice was successful during the reign of Diocletian and provided the empire with more efficient government and defence against foreign attacks.

But the establishment of the tetrarchy had a bearing on another problem, the elevation and stabilization of the imperial office within the realm. Diocletian had supposed that the system of two superior rulers, seconded by their caesars and heirs, would largely put an end to usurpation by the ambitious. More significant in the attempt to create respect for imperial authority was the orientalization of the monarchy. This orientalization had been going on throughout the third century, and could be seen in the puerile efforts of Elegabalus or in the coinage of emperors such as Geta and Aurelian. Moreover, certain elements of absolute monarchy had long been present in Greek political tradition. In later times Justinian traced the origins of imperial sovereignty to the action of the Roman senate in 24 BC freeing the augustus from the compulsion of the laws and thus transferring sovereignty from the people to the ruler. But if even in this earlier period there was a divine element behind the *auctoritas* of the augustus, it was in the third century that the *princeps* was transformed into an Oriental, divine, absolute monarch. Diocletian's arrangements completed the transformation. 'Proskynesis' or 'adoratio' (the eastern ceremony of genuflection addressed to divinity), purple robes, jewelled diadems, belts, and sceptres became permanent parts of the imperial tradition. The emperor, ruler by divine grace, was the sole fount of law. Seclusion of the monarch, an

Oriental practice by which the person of the ruler was removed from contact with the profane, was carefully balanced by the splendid official ceremonials, at which his power and glory were displayed to the citizens and courtiers. Constantine's conversion to Christianity, it is true, necessitated an adaptation of the imperial cult to the demands of a stringent monotheism. But the adaptation which resulted, Byzantine kingship, was to all purposes the same as that which emerged under Diocletian. The emperor (as the friend of Christ) and his empire (as a reflection of the heavenly kingdom) were divinely inspired and protected. The Oriental ceremonies attendant upon court ritual remained one of the most characteristic of all Byzantine practices.

Administratively and militarily the measures of Diocletian and Constantine were calculated to facilitate internal control and defence from foreign attacks. But the chief threat to imperial power was internal rather than external, and this problem was given preference. The greatly expanded bureaucratic apparatus was centralized in the imperial consistory, made up of the highest financial and administrative officials of the court, who addressed the emperor not only on routine administrative matters, but on high policy as well. In the provinces the reforms of Diocletian and Constantine weakened potential rebels by removing heavy concentrations of power from the hands of officials. As the power of any given official was directly related to the size and wealth of the area which he governed, the provinces were doubled in number and their size reduced. More radical were the complementary measures by which civil and military authority were thenceforth separated in such a manner that ambitious provincial officials who might contemplate rebellion were effectively hamstrung.

Nevertheless, the problem of defence against Persians and Germans meant that military considerations were not far behind considerations of imperial centralization. The old traditional military frontiers and policies of the Roman past were maintained. The emperor repaired the old border fortresses and town walls, new forts were built, and the *limitanei* (or frontier militia) retained their defence stance on the Rhine, Danube, and Euphrates. But as this older arrangement was no

4, 5 Gold *aureus* of Diocletian, struck at 60/lb., as can be seen on the reverse (right)

longer sufficient to contain the attacks of Germans and Persians the military principle of defence in depth was adopted. The emperors created mobile field armies stationed in the heartland of the provinces rather than on the borders. Such armies in Anatolia or the central Balkans could protect provincial life from pillaging barbarians who had broken through the frontiers or be used to reinforce the borders. In the capital, new forces were added to the crack imperial troops who accompanied the emperor. Even within the armies, however, the principle of separation of powers, which sought to protect the emperor from insubordination, was operative, and superior command of cavalry and infantry was divided.

The reforms of the late third and early fourth centuries greatly increased state expenditure on account of the considerable increase in military and bureaucratic personnel. This situation caused Lactantius to complain that the number of beneficiaries had begun to grow greater than the number of taxpayers, and the increased financial outlay at the end of the century proved to be more than the already strained economy could bear. Debasement of the coinage and inflation in the preceding period had created havoc with government salaries (which were largely fixed) and with prices. The famous edict of prices (AD 301) bears witness to the government's concern and also to its failure to fix the cost of living. If the state were to survive, it was imperative that its economic life be brought into harmony with harsh reality, and this is precisely what Diocletian

6, 7 The reformed coinage. Gold *solidus* of Constantine, struck at 72/lb., as indicated on the reverse

accomplished. Realizing the inadequacy of the taxes which the government collected in cash, Diocletian developed the old levies in kind, the *annonae*, which had provided the armies with their physical necessities. The *annona*, formerly an extraordinary tax, was henceforth applied to the rural population on an annual basis.

The new system of taxation freed the government from the vicissitudes of monetary debasement and price fluctuations, for it now paid its officials and troops largely in foodstuffs and clothing. It also forced the government to keep the peasants on the soil to cultivate it and necessitated systematic assessments of the arable land, types of agricultural production, and population. The tax apparatus which arose was to have a long life in the Byzantine empire and was also to affect the tax structure of the Islamic world. The new system enabled the government to formulate an annual budget based on the agricultural produce of the empire. Yet it would seem that Diocletian and Constantine did not intend to abandon completely a money economy. Both instituted coinage reform with the issues of good silver and gold coins. Constantine took the gold coin of Diocletian (struck at 60/lb.) and struck the *solidus* (72/lb.) which was to become the money of international exchange *par excellence* until the eighth century when it would share that distinction with the gold *dinar* of the Arabs. Every five years the traders and craftsmen of the towns, who were free from the *annona*, paid a cash tax known as the *chrysargyron*.

21

It was in the field of religion that the policies of the two emperors contrasted most sharply, for Diocletian remained pagan and Constantine embraced Christianity. The triumph of Christianity is to be understood primarily in terms of two historical facts. First, Christianity was one of those Oriental mystery cults which, as a result of their message and organization, and because of the peculiar conditions of the third-century Roman world, had played an important part in transforming the emotional climate of the Mediterranean lands. The victory specifically of Christianity, rather than of some other Oriental religion, was in large part due to the favour with which Constantine and his successors regarded it. Christianity had existed for some three hundred years prior to Constantine, and yet at the time of Constantine's conversion, it was the religion of a very small minority in the Mediterranean world. Its victory was the result of state support, just as in Sassanid Persia, where the ruler supported Zoroastrianism, Christianity remained a minority religion, and in Egypt and Syria, where Christianity had spread and bloomed, the Arab conquest eventually entailed the decline of Christianity and the spread of Islam. In the same way, the Turkish conquest of Anatolia and the Latin preponderance in southern Italy and Sicily meant the replacement of Greek Christianity by Islam and Catholic Christianity respectively; while perhaps the most interesting example of the principle *cuius regio eius religio* was the Iberian peninsula where Christianity and Islam alternated in consonance with the pulse of Arab and Christian military successes.

From the end of the first century, until Constantine made Christianity the favoured religion, the reward which the state meted out to those who professed Christianity was death. In actual practice, however, though the legal status of Christianity did not change, the Christians were tolerated, and by the end of the second and the early third century they had not only successfully proselytized among the upper classes but had also become an accepted part of the empire's society.

The 'peace' between the Roman state and the Christian Church was, however, violently disturbed by the events of the third century which brought to the throne men of a new breed. These were the soldier-emperors from Illyricum who felt that in order to save the state the old religious practices and ways must be followed.

This revival of Roman paganism reactivated the waning hostility between the state and the Christians. When Decius persecuted the Christians in the years 249–51, it was not so much because he despised Christianity as a religion, but because the Christians refused to sacrifice to the gods, and he felt that the safety of the state could only be assured by prayers to the gods. Thus the Decian persecution was politically, rather than religiously, motivated. The Illyrian emperor Valens renewed discriminatory measures in an effort to destroy the corporate life of the Church. When he fell a victim to the Persians, the Christians could rejoice at their good fortune and Gallienus promptly returned the confiscated Church property. Thereafter state persecution of the Christians ceased until the reign of Diocletian and many Christians entered state service.

Diocletian himself observed the 'peace' with the Christians for the greater part of his reign. Probably he would have been satisfied with the *status quo* had it not been for his caesar Galerius. But the latter, supported by a circle of neo-Platonists, was a determined opponent of the Church and did everything in his power to persuade his augustus to move against the Christians. A series of incidents, rightly or wrongly blamed on the Christians, and the consent of the oracle of the Milesian Apollo, brought Diocletian round to the sentiments of his caesar. The emperor and Galerius issued four edicts between 302 and 305 which revived the state's persecution of the Church. Christian churches, scriptures, and liturgical books were to be destroyed; Christians were henceforth forbidden to assemble and were placed outside the law; and all men, women, and children who refused to sacrifice were to be put to death. Many abandoned their profession of Christianity because of the fearful persecutions, but such a great number remained steadfast that they filled the prisons and jails, with the result that there was no room for criminals. In 303, when Diocletian celebrated his vicennial in Rome, he ordered that all the jailed Christians be forced to sacrifice so that the prisons might be emptied. Actually Galerius abandoned the persecution in 311, as a result of a fatal illness which he believed to be the vengeance of the Christian God, and surprisingly issued an edict of tolerance. But the status of Christianity became definitive only when Constantine removed his political rivals, Maxentius in 312, and Licinius in 324. Anxious over the issue of the conflict with Maxentius, Constantine was satisfied that the Christian God had indicated His support in the approaching struggle. The appearance of the cross in the heavens with the legend 'In this shalt thou conquer', and the vision in which Christ instructed Constantine to manufacture the labarum, instilled Constantine with a confidence in Christ's support which later seemed to him justified by the results. The emperor did not immediately accept the exclusive nature of Christianity; but the clergy were so pleased with the new turn of events that they did not object to the pagan practices which Constantine continued.

It was, of course, his defeat of Maxentius in the battle of the Milvian Bridge which marked the beginning of the ultimate triumph of Christianity, for even though it did not become the exclusive religion of the state, it now enjoyed imperial preference. Constantine became a lavish patron of the Church, supporting it with generous gifts and privileges, and simultaneously confiscating the treasures of the pagan temples.

The Church had miraculously acquired a generous patron, but it had simultaneously taken on a powerful master. The tradition of the Roman emperor as *pontifex maximus* survived, in a modified form, in Byzantine caesaropapism. Convinced that the unity and survival of his empire depended upon the unity of the Church, Constantine used the imperial power and prestige in an effort to heal the disputes which were now arising among the bishops. In an attempt to heal the Donatist conflict he received petitions from the bishops, called a council, exiled bishops, and made use of persecution. His behaviour in the Arian controversy illustrates how fully developed his caesaropapism was. It was he who initiated the call for an ecumenical council, brought the bishops to Nicaea and maintained them at state expense, presided over and directed the deliberations and enforced upon the bishops the theological solutions which he preferred. As in so many other institutional transformations, Constantine left his indelible mark on the relations of Church and state in the east.

8 Constantine presenting a model of the city to the Virgin; detail of a late tenth-century mosaic in Hagia Sophia ▶

9 Constantine leading his troops in the Battle of the Milvian Bridge in 312; from a ninth-century manuscript

The emperor would remain the master of the Church. Though powerful patriarchs, weak emperors, and exceptional circumstances might temporarily redress the balance in favour of the Church, the survival of a centralized state enabled the emperor to control the Church.

The most apparent manifestation of a change in the established order was the desertion of Rome as the imperial capital. Though Milan replaced it as the imperial centre in the west, the principal imperial residence came to be located in the east, Diocletian establishing himself in Nicomedia, and Constantine in Constantinople. The choice of these two Greek cities indicates that the empire's political centre of gravity had shifted to the east. It was not until the reign of Charlemagne that a political centre of comparable magnitude would crystallize in the west. When Constantine traced the limits of his new city, he was laying the foundations for a metropolis which would become the largest urban concentration in medieval Europe, and which would leave its imprint upon history as few cities have. He decided that the New Rome should be inferior in no way to the Old Rome. He created a senate, provided the citizens with free

10 The Milvian Bridge (Ponte Milvio) today. The battle that took place here was decisive in the history of Christianity

bread and games, and built churches and public buildings on a lavish scale. He plundered the cities and temples of their marbles and statues in order to ornament his new capital.

Historical and geographical forces had made of Rome an ineffective capital. In contrast, Constantinople was strategically located midway between the critical Danubian and eastern frontiers and between the principal military reservoirs of the Balkans and Anatolia. The eastern provinces were more populous than those of the west, and urban and industrial development there was more vital. Commercially the new city enjoyed the best natural harbour of the medieval world. The Golden Horn, protected from the currents and winds, was a deep body of water which could accommodate large numbers of vessels. Located at the junction of water and land routes which connected east and west, south and north, the city was to be the greatest commercial emporium of Europe for many centuries. Chinese silks, eastern spices, Egyptian wheat, slaves from the west, and furs from the north indicate the international character of the market at Constantinople. The waters immediately adjacent to the city were (and still are) a rich fishing ground which yielded

27

11 Constantinople at its greatest extent and prosperity, in the ninth to eleventh centuries.

an ever-ready source of sustenance to the inhabitants and citizens. This location not only provided Constantinople with immense economic vitality, but also made it impregnable. Guarded as it was on three sides by water, and girt by an effective system of land and sea walls, the capital was secure against either land or naval attack. Throughout its long history, the empire was able to survive the virtual loss or at least the occupation of critical provinces by powerful enemies. The inability of the enemies to take this central bastion (with the exceptions of 1204 and 1453) enabled the Byzantines to bide their time until the opportune moment for a successful counter-attack. One final condition which, along with the others, may have persuaded Constantine to found Constantinople was his desire to

In the foreground is the Sea of Marmora; behind the city is the famous Golden Horn

break with the pagan past and to centre the empire in a new Christian foundation.

Constantine's dedication of the new imperial capital in 330 marked the end of half a century of momentous reforms. Those reforms, with their roots in the disorders of the third century, institutionalized the transitional trends in disintegrating Roman society. What emerged has been variously characterized as an absolute monarchy, an Oriental empire, a corporate state. It is undeniable that elements of each were present, for the divinely-ordered *basileus* (emperor) presided over a highly centralized administration which effectively regulated the economic and social life of each subject.

29

The reformed and revitalized empire was to be put to an arduous and violent test by the crisis of the late fourth and fifth centuries. This was precipitated by the fear which the Huns spread among the Goths. These newcomers on the European scene were to be the first of a long line of nomadic conquerors that would terrorize the settled society of the Christian and Muslim worlds. Beginning with the Huns and lasting for a millennium, the continuous strife of the Altaic peoples in the wasteland of central Asia resulted periodically in the westward march of Bulgars, Avars, Patzinaks, Uzes, Cumans, Seljuks, and Mongols. These tribes of the Altai, who had been formed by the geographical, climatic, and political turbulence of central Asia, confronted not only the Byzantines but even the warlike Goths with a military system which was efficient, ruthless, and terrifying.

The Huns, forced to leave central Asia, first appeared in southern Russia where they dispersed the Alans and destroyed the state of the Ostrogoths. Finally they forced the Visigoths to seek refuge in the Byzantine empire after having defeated them at the Dniester River. In 376 the Visigoths petitioned Valens for asylum south of the Danube and the emperor, not realizing the problems which the presence of a whole nation under arms would cause, gave his consent. But when the Visigoths began to enter Byzantine territory, the imperial authorities were simply not equipped to handle the provisioning and policing of the barbarian hosts, and to make matters worse Lupicinus, the *comes* (Count) of Thrace, began to exploit the panic-stricken Goths and enslave their families in return for bread. The angered barbarians ravaged the Balkans and soon Valens faced them with his forces outside Adrianople in 378. The ensuing conflict, in which Valens and perhaps two-thirds of the imperial forces perished, was a shattering defeat for the empire, but the barbarians were unable to exploit their victory, and when they appeared before Adrianople, Perinthus, and Constantinople, the strongly walled Greek cities held them at bay.

The accession of the Spaniard Theodosius I brought an energetic soldier-emperor to the throne who, though not successful in

12 Theodosius (379–95), last emperor of both east and west, presiding over the games at Constantinople; relief on the base of an obelisk, *c.* 390

destroying the Visigothic menace, provided the tottering empire with a badly needed breathing period. Secure in his possession of the walled cities, Theodosius had to restrict the Visigothic raids which were desolating the rural areas. In 382 he formally permitted them to settle in Lower Moesia as federate troops (*foederati*), and as they abandoned Dacia, the Huns occupied it unopposed. Theodosius, evidently an admirer of their martial qualities, took many of the Visigoths into the armies of the empire. But this was a dangerous step, the consequences of which were seen in the history of the next few years. The Visigothic king, Alaric, was able to attain the high office of *magister militum* by simply blackmailing the government with his raids in Thessaly and the Peloponnese. The quarrel between Arcadius, emperor of the east, and Stilicho (the Vandal general who really ruled the empire in the west) over possession of Illyricum greatly improved the prospects of Alaric. For though Stilicho defeated Alaric twice in Greece and twice in northern Italy, because of the quarrel with Arcadius over Illyricum, he refrained from destroying the Visigoths. After the death of Stilicho, Alaric succeeded in ravaging Italy and in sacking Rome (410). This barbarian chief, who had paraded his hordes across the empire under the full light of history, hoped to cross to Africa and settle his followers there. But he died prematurely and one of his successors, Wallia, eventually led the Visigoths northward and settled them in southern Gaul, where the emperor commissioned him to drive from Spain the barbarians who had recently settled there.

These barbarians, the Suevi, Alans, and Vandals, had taken advantage of Stilicho's preoccupation with Alaric in northern Italy and with the province of Illyricum to march through Gaul, ravaging and plundering, and make their way to Spain. Here the Vandal leader Gaiseric received an invitation from the rebellious Byzantine governor of Africa to support him, with the promise, in exchange, of half of the Byzantine provinces in North Africa. In 429 imperial vessels ferried the Vandals and Alans to the African coast, and by 439 Gaiseric had taken Carthage. His audacity grew rapidly with each success, culminating in the sack of Rome (455) and a raid on the distant Peloponnese (465).

13, 14 Rulers of east and west. The Vandal general Stilicho (left) was the real power behind Honorius, the western emperor. Right, marble head presumed to be Arcadius, emperor of the east

15 This mosaic in the Church of S. Apollinare Nuovo in Ravenna shows ships at Classis, the port of that city

The Italian peninsula, largely isolated by the establishment of the Visigoths in the northwest and the Vandals in the south, became an easy prey to another Germanic people, the Ostrogoths. This people had been settled by the imperial government as *foederati* in northern Pannonia on the borders of Italy after the breakup of Attila's empire in 452. When in 476 the German Odovacer deposed the last emperor of the west, the Byzantine ruler Zeno commissioned the Ostrogothic leader Theodoric to invade Italy and to supersede the ruler there '. . . until he should come'. In fact Zeno did not come and by 493 Theodoric had formed the Ostrogothic kingdom. With the establishment of the Burgundians and Franks in Gaul and the Saxons in England, the dismemberment of the empire in the west was complete and a new host of Germanic kingdoms had arisen on the carcass of the empire.

It is significant that the Germanic threat had first appeared, in its most violent form, in the east. Both Visigoths and Ostrogoths had threatened the east; but in spite of their repeated successes, they were forced to move westwards, and although the west resisted, and might perhaps even have prevailed under Stilicho, after his death it collapsed. The reasons for the success of the east are to be sought in its greater material and spiritual resources. The Balkans bore the initial brunt of the *furor Teutonicus*, but the Germans were not able to destroy the wealth and manpower of Anatolia, Armenia, the Caucasus, Syria, and Egypt. The strength which the more developed urban society of the east gave the empire is impressive. This society also successfully resisted the internal penetration of the barbarians which threatened to Germanize the armies and bring the bureaucracy under its control. When the Goths' general Gainas attempted to take over the government in Constantinople, he aroused a nationalism which matched in ferocity that of the nineteenth century. Synesius, a Greek intellectual from the province of Cyrenaica, admonished the emperor that to have Germans in the army was the equivalent of bringing wolves into the sheepfold. Elaborating on the old Hellenic theory that Greeks and barbarians were different in kind and their union unnatural, he suggested that if they could not be sent beyond the Danube whence they had come, they should be put

16 Gold coin of Theodoric the Great, Ostrogothic ruler of Italy, who was nominally the Byzantine emperor's deputy but in fact a powerful independent monarch

to labour in the fields. The Goths of Anatolia, who had sided with Gainas, were defeated by the local inhabitants, and when Gainas and his Goths finally abandoned Constantinople, the citizens slew several thousands of the barbarians as they were departing.

The east had survived because it had the men, the resources, and the will to survive. The west, unequal to the east in manpower and wealth, was further debilitated by the breakdown of the administration and the military machine.

Free of Germans, the east was, however, faced with religious problems which nearly succeeded in destroying it where the Germans had failed, and which were absent in this high degree in the west. Christianity had experienced a remarkable expansion following the conversion of Constantine, for in the century that followed his death, all rulers, save Julian, were dedicated Christians, Furthermore, the evolution of ecclesiastical institutions prior to 312 had endowed Christianity with a well-developed administrative mechanism, the efficiency of which played an important rôle in its resistance to persecution and then its spread. This apparatus, with the episcopacy at the top and descending through the various lower clerical orders, constituted a hierarchic pyramid which the neophyte had to ascend from the bottom in order to attain any high office. Though many of

35

the bishops conceived of their function in the light of the Old Testament, the influence of the imperial administration upon the structure of the Church is obvious.

If, however, the spread of Christianity implied its worldly involvement, reaction to this situation, combined with the asceticism in the New Testament, gave rise to monasticism. The heremitic monasticism of St Anthony and the cenobitic foundations of St Pachomius in Egypt represent the crystallization of these ascetic tendencies within the Church. Though both types of monasticism remained popular in the Byzantine empire, it was fortunate that St Basil adopted the Pachomian version, and this ensured that the energies and power of the monastic movement would contribute to society at large.

A further result of the growth of the Church was the rivalry of certain episcopal sees within the Church structure. One of the great problems of any federation is the difficulty of reconciling the theoretical equality of all members with the realistic fact that obviously some members are more important than others. In the fifth century this rivalry became quite bitter as the bishops of Alexandria and Rome resented the rapid rise in prominence of the bishops of Constantinople, and the Antiochene bishops attempted unsuccessfully to put an end to the pretensions of the episcopate of Jerusalem. Behind the ensuing struggle between the Churches of Constantinople and Rome was the principle that the rank and importance of a bishopric in the ecclesiastical administration depended upon the size and importance of the city in the civil administration. Just

17 St Menas, represented in this sixth-century Coptic ivory box, was an Egyptian martyred during the Diocletian persecutions

18, 19 Profane and sacred aspects of Coptic art. Wool embroidery of a dancer (left);
wall painting of the Virgin and Child (right)

as the bishops of Old Rome had enjoyed a position of ecclesiastical
pre-eminence because Rome had been the capital of the empire, so
now the bishop of Constantinople claimed to enjoy a similar position
because he was bishop of the New Rome. It was in response to these
claims of Constantinople that Pope Damasus expounded the
doctrine of Petrine supremacy in the late fourth century.

The great intellectual achievement of the Church in the fourth and
fifth centuries was the definition of Christianity through the
formulation of a theology. Modern man for the most part considers
theology as little more than the irrelevant speculation of the priestly
caste, neutralized and bypassed by the advance of scientific thought.

37

But Byzantine society was theologically oriented. Theology seems to have been the favourite topic of conversation even with the ordinary citizens of Constantinople. Gregory of Nyssa remarked that when he went to the capital, the citizens were talking unintelligible theology. 'If you ask someone how many obols a certain thing costs, he replies by dogmatizing on the born and unborn. If you ask the price of bread, they answer you, the Father is greater than the Son, and the Son is subordinate to Him. If you ask is my bath ready, they answer you, the Son has been made out of nothing.'

The Greek passion for logic and speculation is abundantly evident in the theological controversies of the period and it might even be said that theology represented a Christian sublimation of these Greek traits. The acts of the first four ecumenical councils are the conclusions which Greek theologians, utilizing Greek logic, extrapolated from Christian teaching. The effort to define Christianity in these councils, however, was as important politically as it was religiously, for it eventually resulted in the disaffection of Syria, Palestine, and Egypt. Thus when Constantine had stated that God demanded the unity and the well-being of the Church as the price for the empire's prosperity, he had been, in a sense, prophetic. For in the Byzantine empire the existence of one emperor, one administration, and one church constituted the bonds which held the multi-national populations together. The Trinitarian controversy, which the Alexandrian priest Arius provoked when he stated that Christ was less than God, consumed theologians and emperors for over half a century. The Council of Nicaea condemned the doctrines of Arius in 325, but since Constantius supported him the government did not renounce the heresy until 381 when Theodosius I called the ecumenical council of Constantinople. Here the theologians formulated the basic creed recited in the majority of Christian churches today. In asserting the full divinity of the Trinity, the bishops condemned a certain Apollonarius of Laodicia, who had declared that Christ was not fully man.

Arianism gradually subsided in the east, but was soon followed by the Christological controversy, and this new debate, arising from the different teachings of the two theological schools of Antioch and

Alexandria, became further complicated by the ecclesiastical ambitions of the various participants. Cyril, the patriarch of Alexandria, launched a bitter attack upon Nestorius, the patriarch of Constantinople, which culminated in the council of Ephesus (431), over which Cyril, supported by his unruly Egyptians, presided. Not surprisingly, he condemned Nestorius, and in so doing, formulated the view that in Christ there occurred the union of two natures, the human and the divine. Though Nestorius himself evidently did not subscribe to the views with which Cyril charged him, the heresy to which he lent his name emphasized the human nature of Christ at the expense of the divine. The other extreme of the Christian position, emphasizing the divine at the expense of the human, was the salient characteristic of the other Christological heresy, Monophysitism. Cyril's Egyptian followers distorted his doctrine of the union of the two natures and declared that though there were two natures before this union in Christ, afterwards there was only one nature, the divine. It was the fourth ecumenical council at Chalcedon which condemned the Monophysite doctrine and insisted upon the completeness of Christ in both his humanity and divinity. The council censured Euytches, the propounder of the Monophysite doctrine, and his supporter, the Alexandrian bishop Dioscurus.

The council of Chalcedon is a major landmark in the ecclesiastical and political history of the world. It completed the definition of Christianity which the councils of the preceding century had commenced, and it elevated the See of Constantinople to a position which overshadowed the Church of Alexandria and which claimed equality with Rome. The decisions of Chalcedon also had political consequences far beyond anything that the participants could have imagined. Monophysitism originated as the position assumed by certain theologians and bishops, but as a result of its spread in Egypt and Syria (those regions which had resisted complete Hellenization), it eventually became associated with non-Greek populations. The toleration which Zeno and Anastasius I accorded Monophysitism enabled it to take such firm root that the emperors of the sixth and seventh centuries vacillated between persecution and compromise in an unsuccessful effort to bring the Monophysites of these provinces

20 Julian the Apostate besieges Ctesiphon, capital of the Sassanid empire, in the campaign of 362–63

back into the folds of the state Church. The long-term political effect of the Christological controversy was the promotion of disaffection and the development of cultural separatism within the empire.

In spite of the formal triumph of Christianity and state sponsorship the Byzantine Church retained a strong missionary spirit. The repeated anti-pagan decrees of Constantine and Theodosius I indicate that paganism was dying a slow death, and the revived opposition of Julian and the Roman senate to Christianity prolonged its existence. In the more isolated areas paganism persisted for many centuries, as was the case in the southern Peloponnese where the Greeks did not receive Christian baptism until the ninth century. Moreover, defeated paganism emerged quite often in the bosom of the Church in the form of heresies. The Church was not able to wean the people away from the pagan practices which had been intimately associated with everyday life, and our own celebrations of 25 December and the New Year, hagiolatry, and other practices are all evidence of the compromises which Christianity had to make. Even today in rural Greece the clergy still oppose the sacrifice of cocks by the peasants on the grounds that it is a pagan practice.

It was, however, in literature and learning that paganism won its most obvious victory. When Christianity spread through the

Graeco-Roman world, it entered a literary and intellectual domain which was superior to that of the Semitic Near East. As Christianity had very little with which to replace Graeco-Roman tradition in this respect, Christian intellectuals were torn between the Christian texts and classical literature. But in order to cope with the Mediterranean world, Christianity had to accommodate itself to the lettered traditions that prevailed there, and the very use of Greek in the New Testament is proof of this necessary accommodation. The Alexandrians, Clement and Origen, created Christian scholarship by adopting Greek critical and philological methods, and the Cappadocian fathers carried the process of acculturation to its logical conclusion. They accepted the value of Greek *paideia* but declared it to be incomplete. Christianity, they proclaimed, was the fulfilment of the *paideia* of the ancients, but they believed that the classics should be studied for their literary form rather than for their content. Christianity did bring new forms in certain respects—in ecclesiastical history, for example, and in hagiography, and hymnography – but the churchmen played a critical rôle in preserving the classics, copying and studying them and writing long commentaries on them. This they did until the end of the empire.

21 St Gregory Nazianzus, one of the four fathers of the eastern Church, and the emperor Theodosius

Justinian (527–65), more than any other ruler, was responsible for establishing the finished forms and setting the tone of the Byzantine society which Diocletian and Constantine had established. His personality and genius inspired and permeated all the great achievements that were accomplished during his long rule. In this respect his rôle in the history of the time was perhaps more important than that of Pericles in fifth-century BC Athens or of Louis XIV in France. Of obscure peasant origins, Justinian nevertheless received an excellent education, and is perhaps the most remarkable example of that social mobility by which obscure but capable individuals could rise spectacularly in the Byzantine empire. Possessed of a lofty conception of his office, Justinian determined to reconstitute the empire territorially, to unify the quarrelling factions in the Church, and to simplify the legal accumulations of the past centuries. The union of these elevated ideals with Justinian's inexhaustible energies (his subjects called him the sleepless emperor) resulted in the reconquest of much of the west, the codification of the law, and a phenomenal artistic accomplishment. His beautiful consort, Theodora, was perhaps of even lower origins (she was the daughter of a bear-tamer at the hippodrome). All agree that she was a powerful personality, and in spite of the rather poor press she received from the prejudiced Procopius, there is no doubt that she had a certain influence over Justinian. In fact the relationship of Theodora and Justinian recalls the association of Pericles and Aspasia. Though Justinian seems to have maintained his own policies in most matters, his determined wife often followed her own desires in such matters as the support of the Monophysite clergy. Perhaps her most decisive act was her intervention in the resolution of the court council that the emperor should flee Constantinople during the Nika rebellion of 532. Had Justinian followed the decision to flee, his reign would have terminated before the consummation of the works for which it is famous.

When the circus factions of the Blues and Greens rioted in January 532 they were carrying on an activity which had long been familiar and dear to the inhabitants of the empire's cities. From at

22 An aristocratic family watching the games at the Hippodrome in Constantinople ▶

23, 24 Mosaic portraits of Justinian and Theodora in the Church of S. Vitale in Ravenna

least the first century sports organizations had existed which were responsible for the games in the hippodromes of the cities. With the passage of time increasing numbers of young men came to be associated with one or another of these circus factions. By the fourth and fifth centuries the competition of the two most important of these, the Blues and Greens, had become so violent that it was accompanied by riots and urban warfare. The factions, however, came to be much more than troublesome sport clubs, for with the barbarian invasions which threatened the cities, the empire armed the *demesmen* (citizens) and thereby converted the factions into an urban militia. In a sense these urban militia sports organizations became the last refuge of the liberties of the empire's cities, and when Byzantine authorities spoke of 'demokratia', they usually had in mind the rebellions and riots of the Blues and Greens. Though the factions usually fought one another, they joined forces and almost overthrew

25 Mosaic in S. Apollinare Nuovo showing the palace of Theodoric with the city of Ravenna in the background

Justinian in the great Nika rebellion of 532. It was during these events that Theodora saved Justinian's throne by urging him to fight to the end. The rebellion, which destroyed a substantial part of the city's centre, was finally defeated in a blood bath during which, contemporaries report, 30,000 perished.

The Nika riots stand as a turning-point of Justinian's reign; after their suppression Justinian embarked upon his reconquest of the west, the rebuilding of the capital, and the completion of the codification of the law.

In spite of the fact that the imperial collapse in the west had been complete, there were certain conditions favourable to the Byzantine reconquest. The indigenous population considered the Goths and Vandals as Arian heretics, whereas the emperor of Constantinople represented the religious establishment. Their settlement in Italy and Africa and their association with a more advanced society had begun to transform many of the barbarian leaders, with the result that the successors of both Theodoric and Gaiseric were somewhat tamer. Finally, the complex system of marriage alliances, which Theodoric had arranged with the Vandal, Thuringian, and Visigothic kingdoms, collapsed and left the Vandals and Ostrogoths diplomatically isolated. After having concluded a peace with the Persians in the east, Justinian sent Belisarius to North Africa in 533. This brilliant general, with only 16,000 men, rapidly put an end to the Vandal kingdom, and by the following year returned to Constantinople where the Vandal king Gelemir and his treasures (which the Vandals had taken from Rome in 455) graced Belisarius' triumph in the hippodrome.

The political situation in Italy greatly facilitated the Byzantine invasion of the peninsula, for not only had the Ostrogoths and Vandals turned against one another (as a result of this the Ostrogoths had, with incredible lack of foresight, permitted the Byzantine fleet to use Sicily as a base for the African expedition), but Queen Amalasuntha had close relations with Justinian. At the same time Byzantine diplomacy had assured papal support by the denunciation in 518–19 of the Henoticon (482) of the emperor Zeno. The Henoticon, an edict of Monophysitic nature, had alienated the papacy and caused a schism between the churches of Constantinople and Rome, which furnished Theodoric with a considerable diplomatic and political advantage in his relations with Byzantium. When the murder of Amalasuntha at the hands of an anti-Byzantine Gothic faction deprived Justinian of his principal pawn, he sent Belisarius to accomplish by arms what diplomacy had failed to do.

The invasion of Sicily in 535 marked the beginning of the reconquest of Italy which was to last for more than two decades and was to devastate the peninsula. The length and difficulty of the campaign was due to the meagreness of the manpower and financial resources which Justinian placed at Belisarius' disposal. The inadequacy of Belisarius' troops (he began the task with only 8,000 soldiers) enabled the Goths to carry on a protracted resistance and often to retake lands and cities from the Byzantines (Rome changed hands five times). Hence it was not until the middle of the century that the eunuch Narses settled the issue favourably, by which time Byzantine arms had also utilized Visigothic dynastic disputes to regain a foothold in Spain.

By exploiting the diplomatic isolation of his opponents in the west and by assuming a defensive stance in the east, Justinian had succeeded in converting the Mediterranean once more into an imperial lake, and the destruction of the two barbarian kingdoms had also brought a temporary lustre to the imperial name. Justinian realized his imperial and Christian ideals not only in the political action of reconquest but also extensively in his architectural and artistic embellishment of the empire. Byzantine art was heavily indebted to Helleno-Oriental developments in Anatolia, Syria and Egypt, but the product which emerged was no servile imitation. It remained faithful to the Christianized Greek spirit and contrasted sharply with Coptic and Syrian art. The political, religious and economic centralization of the empire in Constantinople was decisive in the character of Byzantine art, and the appearance of an inspired monarch with a handful of gifted architects and artists not only induced a crystallization but simultaneously produced the apogee of Byzantine art. Constantinople itself sent forth the architects and plans for churches, civic buildings, and fortifications to its provinces. Even in such a detail as the carving of capitals of columns the domination of Constantinople is reflected, for most such capitals were of a uniform Constantinople type and were hewn from the Proconessian quarries near the capital.

26 Cornice and capitals from the Church of SS. Sergius and Bacchus, built in the reign of Justinian

The Nika riots, by virtue of the extensive destruction which they caused to the capital, enabled Justinian to give full play to his passion for building and to provide the city with architectural monuments worthy of its status as the greatest city west of China.

Constantinople had grown so rapidly after 330 that in the fifth century new land walls had to be built in order to protect the greatly expanded metropolis. As the disturbances of 532 had gutted extensive sections of the district near the palace, including Hagia Sophia and the senate buildings, Justinian determined to rebuild the church on a magnificent scale and for this purpose purchased the remaining houses in order to demolish them. The new church which he con-

28 The Golden Gate and walls of Constantinople

structed ranks, along with the Parthenon and St Peter's in Rome, as one of the three most important buildings in European history, and is the most significant edifice in the religious architecture of eastern Europe and the Near East. Just as in the military realm Justinian was served by competent generals, so too in his building activities he enjoyed the assistance of talented architects, the best known of whom, Anthemius of Tralles and Isidore of Miletus, built this famous church. Justinian assembled marble and stone from the pagan monuments of Athens, Rome, Ephesus and Baalbek, and the quarries of Greece, Egypt, Africa and Asia Minor furnished new marbles. The splendour of the marbles was enhanced by the lavish application of

49

29, 30 Hagia Eirene (above) was built in 532 under Justinian. The Roman tradition of practical civic building was continued by Justinian, during whose reign these underground cisterns (left) were constructed

31 The Aqueduct of Valens, Constantinople, was built in 368 to carry water to the imperial palaces

gold, silver, ivory and semi-precious stones. Justinian and his architects, at the head of several thousand workers, terminated this Herculean labour in the relatively short period of five years.

At the inauguration ceremony of the completed church (27 December 537), the patriarch received Justinian at the church's entrance and thereby initiated a new period in Byzantine ceremonial which was to last within the empire itself until 1453. Justinian entered the church and proclaimed aloud, 'Glory to God who has deemed me worthy of accomplishing such a work! O Solomon! I have vanquished thee!' Architecturally the great accomplishment was the raising of the enormous central dome (thirty-one metres in diameter) which the architects achieved by a series of devices transferring the great weight of the dome successively onto four pendentives and then onto four huge piers. The interplay of the light which entered through the windows in the dome and walls, with the

51

splendid marbles and mosaic decoration, and the spatial arrangement of the building, were to overpower and awe worshippers and observers for a millennium. Justinian supplied the capital with a new senate building, public baths and cisterns, and of course with other churches. Second in importance to Hagia Sophia was the Church of the Holy Apostles built in the form of the Greek cross and surmounted with five domes. In the provinces his artistic efforts are still to be seen as far west as Italy and as far east as Mount Sinai. Finally, the imperial architects of the period girt the frontiers with an extensive network of fortresses in the vain hope of holding the barbarians.

As famous as Hagia Sophia, but more significant historically, was the legal monument which Justinian bequeathed, with the assistance of the untiring Tribonian, to succeeding centuries. Though local practice and law were very much alive, the legal relations of Byzantine society formally rested upon the enormous legal repository which centuries of imperial edicts and the legal opinions of famous lawyers had created. Justinian accompanied the simplification and codification of the law with a reform in the textbooks and instruction of law in the schools.

The patronage of Justinian and the splendour of the age were also reflected in the intellectual activity of the capital and the provinces, an activity which was to be largely centralized in Constantinople after the loss of the eastern provinces to the Arabs. Procopius, in spite of his occasional slanders, is the dominant literary figure. In his history of Justinian's wars he is a worthy continuator of the ancient Greek historiographical traditions. His analysis of the plague which decimated the empire in 542, so closely modelled on its Thucydidean counterpart, is illustrative of the inspiration which Herodotus, Thucydides, and Polybius furnished to Byzantine historiography and which accounts for its superiority to that of the medieval West. Because of this continuity Greek historiography has a record of longevity second only to that of the Chinese. Choricius of Gaza, too, followed the classical pattern in rhetoric by modelling his oratory on that of Demosthenes. In contrast to this archaistic classicism was Justinian's closing of the ancient schools of philosophy in Athens. The greatest of the Byzantine hymnographers, Romanus Melodus,

33, 34 Byzantine craftsmanship at its best. The agate 'Rubens vase' (once owned by the painter), c. 400 (left); and a personification of India (right), a silver plate of the sixth century

composed religious poetry in conformity with the spoken rather than written Greek, whereas the court poet, Paul Silentiarius composed his description of Hagia Sophia in classical hexameters. This development of two languages remained a characteristic of the Byzantine tradition until modern times. The progress of Greek as the official language of the government was well on its way by the end of Justinian's reign, a process which harmonized with reality.

The evolution which took place in the three centuries between Diocletian's accession and Justinian's death had effected dramatic changes in Mediterranean society without causing any drastic and abrupt break with the past. The institutions which this evolution produced had attained political and economic uniformity, but in spite of Justinian's activity they had not succeeded in producing a religious and cultural homogeneity. These disparate elements effectively hindered the integration of Byzantine society and thus greatly weakened it.

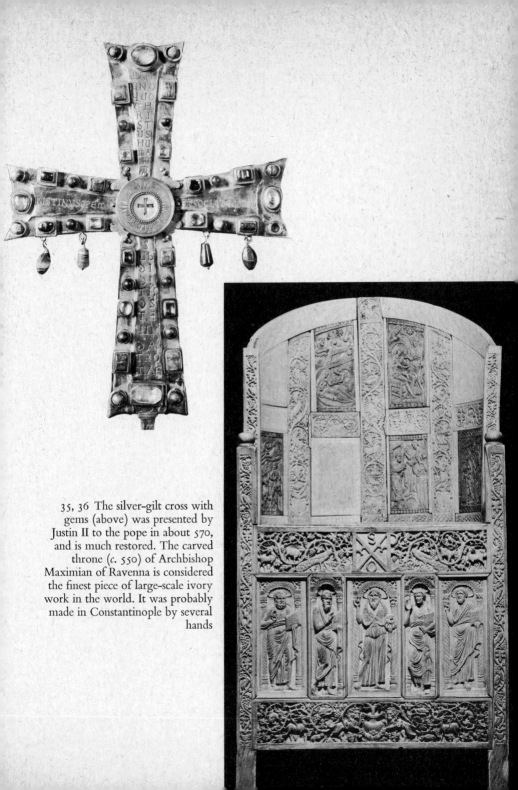

35, 36 The silver-gilt cross with gems (above) was presented by Justin II to the pope in about 570, and is much restored. The carved throne (c. 550) of Archbishop Maximian of Ravenna is considered the finest piece of large-scale ivory work in the world. It was probably made in Constantinople by several hands

37 This *multi-solidus* gold piece (now lost) was minted to celebrate Belisarius'
victory over the Vandals, but shows the glorified emperor Justinian in military dress

II ESTABLISHMENT OF A HOMOGENEOUS BYZANTINE SOCIETY

Retrenchment

Justinian had accomplished his spectacular reconquest of the west at a very high price: the neglect of the Balkan and Asiatic provinces. The most remarkable example of this was the Syrian campaign of the Persian monarch Chosroes who, in 540, sacked the great metropolis of Antioch. This neglect, compounded by the financial exhaustion ensuing from Justinian's grandiose projects, was to bear bitter fruit in the seventh century. Furthermore, the centralizing forces so manifest in the artistic, legal, religious and political programme of Justinian failed to overcome the centrifugal tendencies in the west and above all in the east. The process by which the east disengaged itself from Byzantine Hellenism in the sixth and seventh centuries put the finishing touches to a development which had moved fitfully for a millennium.

It is ironic that the religious differences which became the focal points of strife between Constantinople and the non-Greek eastern provinces ultimately derived from the position of the theological schools of Antioch and Alexandria, both of which schools represented Greek metaphysical traditions. In spite of the condemnation of Monophysitism at Chalcedon (451), the succession of two Monophysite emperors (Zeno and Anastasius I) and the passivity of Justin I provided several decades of conditions favourable to the spread of Monophysitism in Egypt and Syria. Justinian was thus faced with a body of strongly-rooted sectaries and his task of bringing the Monophysites into the Church was further complicated by his need to placate the papacy and by Theodora's unashamed patronage of the Monophysite clergy. Accordingly, there is an extraordinary range and diversity in Justinian's theological actions. He was, variously, a supporter of the decisions of the council of Chalcedon, a Theopaschite, and a Monophysite of the Aphthartodocetist persuasion, as he tried vainly to please one and all.

Monophysitism had the advantage of two very capable leaders in the sixth century who gave the sect articulate form: Severus who formulated Monophysite theology, and Jacob Baradaeus who erected the ecclesiastical structure of the Monophysite Church. In a period when the Chalcedonians occupied many of the bishoprics Jacob ordained Monophysite bishops for the same episcopal sees; and though they were unable to take over the sees to which they were appointed, he thereby created the skeleton of a Monophysite hierarchy which could, under more propitious circumstances, replace the Chalcedonian clergy. The emergence of Monophysitism gave further impetus to the development of Coptic and Syriac as liturgical and literary languages so that by the early seventh century the conflict brewing between Chalcedonian Greeks and Egyptian-Syrian Monophysites was ethnic as well as religious.

The succession of the incompetent and brutal Phocas (602–10) marked the low point of the decline which followed Justinian's death. An almost complete military collapse in the east and the Balkans, bloody repression of the eastern sectaries, and the suicidal strife of the Blues and Greens in the cities were rapidly debilitating and consuming the empire. The papacy alone rejoiced in the rule of the bloodthirsty Phocas. This was Phocas' reward for taking the side of Pope Gregory I who had earlier protested against the assumption by the patriarch of Constantinople of the title oecumenical patriarch. However, the ease with which Heraclius, son of the Armenian exarch of North Africa, put an end to the reign of Phocas indicates that the Byzantines were sickened by him.

When Heraclius arrived in Constantinople the empire's position appeared beyond redemption, for the Avars, with their Slav and Bulgar subjects, were overrunning the Balkans, and the Persians were advancing through the eastern provinces, until in 615 they had actually occupied Egypt, Syria, and Palestine. The Persians subjected Jerusalem to massacre and fire, carrying off to Ctesiphon the Holy

Cross and the patriarch; and in Egypt a Coptic governor now ruled the land under the aegis of Persia. With the encampment of the Persian armies under Shahen on the Bosphorus, Heraclius was virtually cut off from the principal sources of manpower and revenues in the greater part of the Balkans and the Near East. But Constantinople, protected by God, the Virgin, and its impregnable mural and maritime defences, remained inviolate. So long as the enemy could not capture this nerve centre, the empire possessed in Constantinople a remarkable vehicle of regeneration. The wisdom of Constantine the Great in choosing this site for his capital was to be proved many times in the history of Byzantium.

Heraclius, however, found the situation so hopeless that he decided to abandon Constantinople for Carthage where his family enjoyed prestige and where eight decades of Byzantine rule had restored economic prosperity. But accident intervened. The ship which had been loaded with the palace treasures sank in a storm, and the patriarch Sergius bound the emperor by oath not to abandon the capital and offered the treasures of the Church to the state. Heraclius now concentrated on building up his military strength, postponing any move against the Persians until the day after Easter in 622 when he sailed from Constantinople to Issus and there began a series of gruelling campaigns that were to last until 628.

38, 39, 40 Imperial portraits: gold *solidus* of Phocas (probably issued in 603); *solidus* of Heraclius (between 613 and 629), shown with his son, afterwards Constantine III; and a later *solidus* of Heraclius (between 629 and 631), now with a heavy beard and moustache, and grown-up son

This Perso-Byzantine war, accompanied by feverish religious passions and hatreds, is perhaps the first full-fledged crusade of the Middle Ages. The poet-chronicler, George of Pisidia, casts the emperor in the rôle of pious fighter for the faith as he describes how, on the eve of the first encounter between Heraclius and the Persian Shahr Barz in the Anti-Taurus,

> Cymbals and all kinds of music gratified the ears of Shahr Barz and naked women danced before him, while the Christian emperor sought delight in psalms sung to mystical instruments, which awoke a divine echo in his soul.

In 623, while campaigning in Azerbaijan, the Byzantine troops systematically destroyed the fire temples of the Persians in city after city. In particular they destroyed Thebarmes, supposed birthplace of Zoroaster, in revenge for the Persian desecration of Jerusalem.

The great crisis came when the Avars laid siege to Constantinople in 626. Chosroes sent Shahr Barz with a new army to co-operate with the Avars in besieging the capital, and ordered Shahen (under pain of death) to hunt down Heraclius in the east. The emperor, refusing to abandon Anatolia and the gains he had made in four years of campaigning, set out for Azerbaijan where he received assistance from the Khazar khan. Meanwhile the siege of Constantinople was pushed forward throughout the month of July, at the end of which time the Avar khan arrived; but his great assault on the land walls was repulsed, it is said by a miraculous icon of the Virgin. All further efforts by both Avars and Persians failed before the spirited defenders (Constantinople was defended by only about 12,000 men) and finally the siege was abandoned. The composition of the famous Akathistos hymn (still sung in Orthodox churches during the Easter season) is traditionally associated with the patriarch Sergius and this successful defence of the city.

The end came in 627 when Heraclius inflicted a decisive defeat on the Persian forces in the region between Nineveh and Gaugamela where a thousand years earlier Alexander had destroyed the Achemenid empire. In 628 the Sassanids, their power broken, sued for

41 The emperor Heraclius (610–41), son of the governor of North Africa, who replaced the incompetent and brutal Phocas. He saved Byzantium from the Persians, only to see the Arabs sweep away his Middle Eastern and North African possessions

peace and relinquished all their conquests. Heraclius returned to Constantinople where he was received by the patriarch Sergius and the Holy Cross, recently recaptured, was raised in a joyous ceremony. A year later the emperor, accompanied by his family, journeyed to Jerusalem where he restored the Cross. Heraclius must have looked back to the year 622 as the turning-point not only in his personal fortune but in that of the empire. He could not know that this same date marked the reversal of fortune in the life of another man, a Semite of Arabia, who also abandoned his own city of Mecca, to go forth to a battle for dominion over men's souls and minds.

The restoration of Byzantine power in the east was temporary and Heraclius himself saw the beginning of its collapse. The immense exertion which had led to his spectacular victory over the Sassanids simultaneously depleted the empire and contributed further to the weakness arising from sectarian and cultural pluralism. Heraclius and his successors made continued attempts to compromise with the Monophysites in a desperate effort to maintain some kind of internal cohesion in the critical areas. From 626 onward Sergius and Heraclius appealed to the Armenians and Syrians by enunciating the doctrine that, though Christ was both human and divine, He was possessed of only one energy. When this doctrine met with opposition from Chalcedonians the patriarch and emperor shifted their ground and declared in the Ecthesis (638) that Christ had one will (Monothelitism). But the results were no more satisfactory. As late as 648 the emperor Constans II attempted to hold the conflicting parties together by forbidding discussions of energies or wills in his Typicon, but again to no avail. When, in 680–81, the sixth ecumenical council condemned Monophysitism and Monothelitism and asserted two wills and two energies without division, alteration, separation, or confusion, Monophysitism was no longer a political problem. The Arabs, in conquering Egypt, Syria, Palestine and Armenia, had removed the Monophysites from the empire and relegated the question to the realm of academic theology. So long as the emperors had hopes of saving the eastern provinces they tried to satisfy the Monophysites; now it was no longer necessary.

The threat of Islam

The Arab conquests of the seventh century, which so altered the historical development of Europe and the Middle East, are as inexplicable and startling to us today as they were to the Byzantines. The new religion which the prophet Muhammed preached transformed much of Arabian society by providing it with religious bonds of unity and an *élan vital* which had previously been lacking. The Arabs had also acquired considerable knowledge of the outside world, whether as mercenaries of the Byzantines and Persians or as merchants in the carrying trade between the Mediterranean and the

Indian Ocean. When the Arabs finally spilled out of the Arabian peninsula they found the Byzantines not yet recovered from the Persian struggle and suffering from the internal convulsions of religious discord. The Persians, defeated by the Byzantines, had in addition suffered from a fossilized social structure that resulted in the *jacquerie* and communism of the Mazdakites.

Soon after the death of Muhammed (632) the Arabs began to raid the regions of both empires immediately to the north. Their attacks on Byzantine territory culminated in the battle of the Yarmuk (636), a crushing defeat for the Byzantines, which settled the fate of Syria and Palestine, though the Hellenic centres of Jerusalem and Caesarea did not fall until 638 and 640. The Chalcedonian patriarch of Jerusalem, Sophronius, received the caliph Umar in Jerusalem and served as his guide to the principal holy sites. The most uncompromising opponent of Heraclius' attempt to placate the Monophysites with Monothelitism, Sophronius reaped the rewards of his obstinacy when he witnessed Umar reverently kneeling in the precinct of the Church of the Resurrection. This sight moved Sophronius to remark: 'The abomination of the desolation which was spoken of by Daniel the prophet is in the holy place.' In 637 the Arab armies defeated the Persians at Kadesiya, in 640 Amr ibn al-As invaded Egypt and one year later the acquisition of Syria, Palestine and Iraq was completed by the conquest of Mesopotamia. In less than a decade a little-known people had with ease terminated a millennium of Graeco-Roman rule in the Near East and had settled the fate of the Sassanid state.

The critical phase of the struggle between Byzantium and the new Islamic giant took place in the reign of Constantine IV (668–85), when the ambitious caliph Muawiyya set out to take Constantinople. He sent his armies repeatedly into Asia Minor and, in a phenomenal display of adaptation, created an Arab naval power which soon occupied Cyprus, Rhodes, Chios and Cyzicus. His forces first besieged Constantinople in 669, but the major effort of the Arabs came in the five-year period 674–78. The Arab fleet based at Cyzicus and the armies which marched across Anatolia tried to storm the powerful bastion, but in vain, and both the Arab fleet and army

42, 43 The Islamic coin (below), bearing an adaptation of a Christian cross on steps, indicates the extent of Byzantine cultural penetration. Right, Mecca as it appeared in 1800; the windowless building in the centre is the Ka'ba

suffered a humiliating disaster in which the dreaded Greek fire invented by a Greek from Syria made its debut. Constantine IV had providentially equipped his fleet with siphons for propelling the secret weapon, and Greek fire became one of the most dreaded weapons of the imperial fleets. This Byzantine victory was crucial for the history of both Christendom and Islam, far more so than the victory of Charles Martel at Poitiers (732). The empire was able to overcome the greatest military effort of Islam and thus to preserve the Christian character of European civilization. The defeat of Muawiyya turned the Arab power back to the Middle East whence it had come, and though the Arabs succeeded in taking Spain, Islamic civilization was eventually confined to non-European areas.

In contrast to Syria, Palestine and Egypt where the Arabs had found a predominantly Monophysite and non-Greek population, Anatolia and the European provinces represented a predominantly

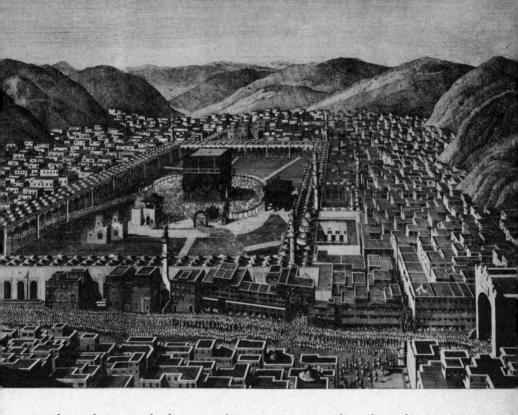

Greek-speaking Orthodox population. Consequently when the rapid advance of the Arabs halted on the borders of Anatolia and at the maritime borders of the Mediterranean islands, the geographic, political and ethnic boundaries coincided. Asia Minor remained an integral part of the empire, intimately involved in the annual raids and counter-raids of the two sides, while the Arab maritime advance halted with the conquest of Crete and Sicily in the ninth century.

The emergence of Islamic power, monopolizing Byzantine military efforts, was the ultimate cause for Byzantium's loss of the west. In this sense the Arab invasion did result in the disruption of the unity in the old Mediterranean world. When the Arabs occupied the Byzantine territories, however, they adopted the urban civilization of Damascus and Antioch, of Jerusalem and Alexandria, so that Byzantine social, economic and cultural institutions continued after the conquest. But in the political realm there was a sharp break between the Islamic and Christian portions of the Mediterranean. Furthermore, it was the Arab invasions which led the papacy to turn its back on Constantinople and to face northwest Europe, thus beginning the policy which led to the alienation of east and west.

The new Western empire

Less than half a century after Narses had re-established Byzantine rule in Italy, the Lombards conquered most of the peninsula. Although the emperors did not neglect Italy (Constans II even made an expedition to Italy in 663 in an effort to expel the conquerors) their life-and-death struggle with the Arabs and Bulgars made it virtually impossible for them to check the Lombards. Differences between the Churches of Constantinople and Rome appeared early because of the swift rise of the former as the most important of the eastern patriarchal seats, and by the eighth century the Iconoclastic controversy exacerbated relations. Nevertheless, the popes relied upon the emperors for protection against the troublesome Lombards. But the fall in 751 of Ravenna, the centre of the Byzantine exarchate in central Italy, and the inability of Constantine V to halt the Lombards because of his intensive military campaigns against the Bulgars and the Arabs, isolated the papacy. The result was that three years later Pope Stephen II journeyed beyond the Alps to meet the Frankish ruler Pepin – a step which started the famous partnership between the Carolingians and the papacy and culminated in Charlemagne's coronation by the pope in Rome on 25 December 800.

44 Constantine V 'Copronymous' (741–75), under whom the persecution of icon-worshippers reached its height

45 Irene, widow of Leo III, was the only woman who ruled the empire on her own (797–802). She did little to enhance its power or prosperity, but re-introduced for a time the worship of icons

This act deeply disturbed the Byzantines because it violated the principle of one empire, and they attempted to oppose Charles' usurpation. But in the hostilities which ensued Constantinople was forced to concede to Charlemagne the title of Basileus in 812. There was now an empire of the east and one of the west as well, and the Byzantine monopoly was broken. The emergence of the western empire is the most spectacular moment in the rise of a new society in western Europe. Just as the genius of Justinian had marked the emergence of Byzantine civilization in the sixth century, so the figure of Charlemagne helped to mould the civilization of western

67

Europe which began to take shape in his time. As the centuries passed the two societies grew apart in political, social, economic, cultural and spiritual life and their separate development is the basis of the difference between western and eastern Europe in modern times. By causing the papacy to seek out the Carolingians the Arab successes in the east played an important rôle in laying the foundation of western European culture. It was also other peoples of the east, the Mongols and the Turks, who at a later period effectively isolated the peoples of Byzantine culture from the culture of the west, and so sharpened the differences which are so apparent in the history of Europe during early modern times. Thus the impact of the Orient, Islamic and Altaic, has been one of the decisive factors in the whole development of east and west in Europe.

Disorder in the Balkans

In the Balkan regions Justinian's neglect coincided with the mounting demographic pressure of new peoples. The lands to the south of the Danube, areas of pillage and raiding since the fourth century, had been occupied by Visigoths, Ostrogoths, Huns, Gepids, and Heruli, who had desolated the northern half of the peninsula, so that by the sixth century when the Slavs and Bulgars settled there they effected a major ethnographic change. The Slav and Bulgarian tribes which had made their way to the Danubian shores early in the sixth century took advantage of Justinian's pre-occupation with the west to cross the borders and to raid imperial territory almost unopposed. The Bulgars invaded the Balkan peninsula in 540, ravaged Thrace, Macedonia, Illyricum, and pressed south as far as Corinth. The Sklavenoi similarly invaded Illyricum in 548, their raid culminating in the sack of Dyrrachium on the Adriatic. Their failure before the walls of Thessalonica two years later was the first in a long series of attempts by both Slavs and Bulgars to break out into the Aegean, and the loss of the city would have entailed serious consequences for Byzantine control in the Greek peninsula. The pressure of the barbarians over the years was such that the Thessalonicans attributed their salvation to the miraculous intervention of St Demetrius, their patron saint.

The Altaic people known as Kotrigurs invaded the Byzantine districts in 559, reaching Thermopylae in central Greece and the environs of Constantinople in the east. Justinian himself and the populace of the capital were panic-stricken, for there were no armies with which to defend the city. Fortunately Belisarius, who had been disgraced by the jealous emperor, hastily gathered a group of peasants and horses and succeeded in terrifying and driving off the Kotrigurs.

Thus, for the greater part of Justinian's reign the Balkans were the scene of activity of various Slavic and Altaic tribes which raided the land sporadically without any overall supervision or direction. The appearance of the Avars on the Danube in 561 altered the situation radically. The Avars, like their predecessors the Huns, were an Altaic people who had abandoned the Asiatic steppe under the pressure of the newly-formed Oguz empire. Desiring lands in the empire and having been refused by Justinian, the newcomers set out to take them by force. Much as the Huns had made military vassals of the Germans, so the Avars subjugated the Slavs and Bulgars and utilized their manpower in the conflict with Byzantium. The emperor Maurice temporarily halted the threat when for the last time he re-established the Danube as the imperial boundary in 599–600. But the rebellion of the army at the prospect of lengthy campaigns in the inclement Balkans followed by the chaotic rule of Phocas (602–10) decided the fate of the northern and central Balkans. The barbarians poured into the peninsula, destroyed Byzantine authority and began to settle on the land in great numbers. With the capture of the principal urban centres in the north, the newcomers destroyed the focal points of the Church and the administration in provinces which had previously suffered depopulation. Thus the invasions not only resulted in a drastic ethnographic transformation, but also obliterated Christianity and Byzantine civilization. Two and a half centuries were to elapse before the elements of Byzantine culture could again be introduced in the area now occupied by the Slavs and Bulgars.

Though the Avars succeeded in occupying much of the Balkans and even in taking the towns of the north, the walled urban centres of Thrace and Greece proved to be the final obstacle to their success.

Nevertheless, with their Slav and Bulgar auxiliaries they seriously threatened Thessalonica and Constantinople in the early seventh century and once more the fate of Byzantine civilization hung in the balance. Thessalonica, in particular, was exposed to the invading hordes because of its strategic location midway between Constantinople and southern Greece. The plight of the empire is dramatically recounted in the miracula of St Demetrius, the city's patron saint:

> Under the episcopate of John the people of Sklavenoi arose, an immense people composed of Drogouvites, Sagoudates, Velegazites, Vaiounites, Verzites, and other peoples. Having made and armed ships of a single tree trunk, they ravaged all Thessaly, the neighbouring isles and the isles of Helladicon, the Cyclades, all Achaea, Epirus, the majority of Illyricum and part of Asia, leaving behind them all of the cities and eparchies as deserts.

At this time, also, the Avars and their followers made a great effort to reduce Thessalonica in a siege which endured for thirty-three days. Thanks to the energies of its archbishop and also to the strength of the city walls, the city, flooded with refugees who had managed to flee from various parts of the Balkans, survived the attacks.

With their failure before Thessalonica and their even more dramatic defeat before the walls of Constantinople in 626, the Avar threat disappeared. The Bulgars and Slavs shortly escaped from Avar tutelage and the Bulgarian khan Kubrat established the Bulgars in the regions of the northern Vardar. During this period the rearguard of the Slav invaders, the Croats and Serbs, also entered the Balkans. Their settlements were of course densest in the northern Balkans, but Slavs settled extensively in parts of Greece as well. It was the less numerous Bulgars, however, who became the most powerful group politically. Constantine IV suffered a military defeat at their hands in 680, and was forced to cede the lands north of Mount Haemus to the khan Asperuch, though the empire enjoyed a respite during the reign of Constantine V who crushed the Bulgars in repeated campaigning. But the recklessness of Nicephorus I, which led to his death and the defeat of his army in the mountainous passes of northern Bulgaria, enabled the Bulgarian ruler Krum to establish the Bulgarian state on firm foundations.

The centuries of barbarian invasions and the disastrous policy of Justinian and of some of his successors produced a completely new ethnographic and political pattern in the Balkans. The ninth-century map of the Balkans indicates how complete this change was. There were Croats in the west, Narentines in Dalmatia, Serbs and Bulgars in the north and east, and finally numerous Slavs who had settled in Greece where, however, they were eventually absorbed by the indigenous population.

Administrative change

The pressure to which the repeated blows of the barbarian peoples subjected Byzantium not only resulted in great losses but also stimulated great internal change and readjustment. This internal evolution indicates that even though Byzantine statecraft never conceived the possibility of altering the framework of autocracy, it was nevertheless capable of great institutional adaptability and resilience. For centuries the administration had been based on Diocletian's separation of civil and military authority, and this arrangement had given the empire respite from rebellion. But the new situation, in which external forces threatened Byzantium with destruction, demanded effective military action. The separation of civil and military power, because of the paralysis of action which it entailed, had to be abandoned. The invasion of the Lombards and the incessant raids of the Berbers had prompted the emperor Maurice to reunite political and military authority in each area in the hands of one individual, the exarch of Ravenna and the exarch of Carthage. Thus began the militarization of the provincial administration, a process which was to lead to extensive social change as well. The process was carried further when, at the time of the Persian invasions of the early seventh century, Heraclius decided to militarize the administration in those Anatolian districts which were still controlled by the empire. As a result the *strategos* (general) of a *theme* (province) became the supreme official in both the military and civil life of his *theme*. Furthermore, the creation of a *theme* entailed the settlement of troops in that particular province, who were supported by gifts of land. Henceforward the performance of military duty by the soldiers of the *themes* and their enjoyment of their freehold lands became inseparable.

The Arab conquests and the invasions of the Slavs and Bulgars led to a further development and extension of the thematic system, and eventually the militarization of provincial government came to comprehend the whole of the empire. Because of the loss of the major part of the Balkans, the *themes* of Anatolia became the principal recruiting ground of the Byzantine army, which they remained for the next four centuries. There is no doubt that the new administrative establishment was of great benefit to the empire for it actually created a new peasant army. The peasant soldiery, with its small landholdings from which it derived the wherewithal to equip itself, provided each province with an indigenous army ready at all times to meet the foe. The appearance of this new 'national' army was matched by a corresponding decline in the prominence of the foreign mercenaries who had been so conspicuous an element in the Byzantine armies during preceding centuries. The loyalty of the latter had never gone far beyond their pay, whereas that of the new peasant-soldier derived from emotional as well as economic sources. Furthermore, the elevation of a section of the peasantry into a military class, together with government support of the peasant as a free landowner and thereby a strengthening of the peasant class as a whole, helped greatly to revitalize the empire's social structure. For in the centuries that followed, the emperors were able to restrict the power of the great landed magnates by supporting and utilizing the peasantry. The amelioration of the conditions of the peasant class was also a great boon to the imperial fisc as the peasants assumed a considerable portion of the tax burden.

Iconoclasm

If the invasions of Arabs, Slavs, and Lombards constituted a crisis for the body of the empire, the Iconoclastic controversy may be

46 The Bulgars' invasion of Byzantine territory; illustrations in a twelfth-century Slavonic manuscript. In the lower half, Krum, king of the Bulgars, is ▶ taunting the captured emperor Nicephorus I

 НИКНФОРЪ ЦРЬ НДЕ НА БЛЪГАРЫ

КРȢМЪ КНАЗЪ ХВАТИ НИКНФОРА ЦРѢ
Н ОСѢЧЕ ГЛАВȢ ЕГО

47, 48 Iconoclasm. A coin of Justinian II (left) still bears the head of Christ. Right, the emperor Leo III (717–41), who launched the attack on icons

described as a crisis of the empire's soul. The quarrel over the admissibility of images in religious art erupted in the eighth century. By the time when Leo III began to attack the use of images as idolatrous, the importance of icons in Byzantine piety and art quite paralleled the Graeco-Roman reverence for and attachment to religious statues. The struggle between the Iconoclasts and the defenders of the icons became so vicious that it consumed society for more than a century. The Church's admission of the image in religious art during the third and fourth centuries was of momentous importance, for had the Church not done so the Graeco-Roman artistic traditions would have largely expired and European art would possibly have taken a course similar to that of Islamic art. But in spite of the Church's acceptance of these traditions there appeared early a voice in the Church which condemned images because they were related to pagan practice, and because their use contravened the Mosaic prohibition of the graven image. Nevertheless, an intensification of the cult of icons was discernible in the latter half of the sixth century when the disintegration of political affairs induced men to hope for miracles, magic and superhuman intervention. As the older tendency of the Greek and Hellenized populations to associate magical powers with physical images reasserted itself, the leaders of society did nothing to suppress it. Rather they promoted this development by such official acts as canon 82 of the council of 692 (which ordained that henceforth Christ might no longer be represented as a lamb but only as a human) and the placing of Christ's image on the coins minted under Justinian II.

The reaction against the use of icons came to a head in 726 when Leo III (a Syrian by orgin), at the urging of certain bishops and after a volcanic eruption which he thought to be the result of God's anger, forbade their use as idolatrous. Their removal and destruction provoked a violent reaction against Leo in many quarters. The empire and papacy severed relations, the *theme* of Hellas revolted, and a cleric safely domiciled in the distant lands of the caliphate wrote a series of theological tracts defending the images. John of Damascus established the basic theological position of Orthodoxy in supporting the icons and successfully defended their use against the

49 An Iconoclast whitewashing an image

50 The Iconoclasts substituted symbols for images. This cross, replacing the apse mosaic, survives in Hagia Eirene

charges of idolatry. It was the Incarnation, he reasoned, which justified the making of images, for thus one can depict the human aspect of Christ. Further, the use of images could not be condemned on the grounds that pagans had also used physical likenesses of their gods, for on the same grounds one would have to condemn Christian exorcism and other practices. Finally, the icon was a record of past events, an imitation (just as man was made in the image of God), and was related to its prototype in a neoplatonic manner. The proper attitude of the beholder of the icon was respect and not, as the Iconoclasts had charged, worship.

The programme of the Iconoclasts attained its greatest successes under the vigorous son of Leo. Constantine, slanderously nicknamed Copronymous (Dung-name) by his outraged opponents, carried the attack to the heart of resistance by waging open warfare on the monastic establishments. He confiscated their properties, martyred some of the monks, drafted others into the army, and forced many to marry nuns. On the theological plane he shifted the Iconoclastic arguments from the charge of idolatry and entered the realm of Christological controversy at the council of Hieria in 754. All who painted or worshipped images were either Nestorians or Monophysites because the human and divine natures of Christ were inseparably united. Anyone who believed he could depict the human Christ was a Nestorian; if he believed that it was the divinity, he was not only a Monophysite but had also violated the uncircumscribability of God. Constantine's own theology was, however, slightly Monophysitic for he tied Christ's humanity so closely to His divinity that He could not be pictorially depicted. The basic positions of both sides were thus formed by the middle of the eighth century, but the conflict continued after the reign of Constantine in a less acerbated form. The seventh ecumenical council of Nicaea restored the icons temporarily in 787, but their final restoration took place only in 843. The controversy, though of Christological significance, was of broader importance because, in assuring the continuity of the Graeco-Roman tradition in Byzantine art, the Hellenic spirit triumphed over this Judaic concept which would have given Byzantine society a more Oriental coloration. Byzantium thus withstood both Oriental military and intellectual advances.

51 The empress Theodora, last of the Macedonian dynasty, restoring icons

52 Though the eastern territories had never been fully Hellenized, Byzantine influences are often evident in their art, for example in the Virgin's features in this sixth-century Syrian ivory panel

Cultural changes

The seventh century was, in many ways, the 'Dark Age' of Byzantium, for aside from the great losses which the empire suffered, there is also a void in contemporary literary remains. The Arab conquests had resulted in the loss of the Near East and North Africa, while the Slavs and Bulgars had occupied most of the Balkans. These tremendous losses had deprived the Byzantines of the important Balkan and Armenian military recruiting grounds, as well as the fruits of

Syrian industry and Egyptian agriculture. The loss of such great cities as Antioch, Damascus, Alexandria and Carthage altered the polycentric character of the empire, and Constantinople remained the sole urban centre of great size; thus Byzantine society became further centralized. This is markedly reflected in artistic and literary developments wherein John of Damascus represents the last afterglow of Byzantine cultural achievement in the lost provinces. The Greeks, Copts and Syrians of the lost provinces were now integrated into the Arab caliphate and subjected to a different culture. It is rather startling that the Egyptian and Syrian Christians, who resisted Hellenization by rejecting the decisions of the council of Chalcedon and developing their own languages, were none the less slowly absorbed by the new masters of the Near East. The Arabization and Islamization of these peoples is one of the truly remarkable cultural phenomena in the history of mankind. The appearance of the Arabs on the eastern and southern shores of the Mediterranean led them to create a seapower which forced the Byzantines to share a condominium over the eastern waters, while commercially, the profitable carrying trade between the Far East and the Mediterranean now fell into Arab hands.

53 Arabization in the provinces lost to Byzantium during the seventh century had a decided effect on the later art style. Even Christian subjects, such as this Nativity from a Syriac Gospel of c. 1216, show an eastern (perhaps Persian) influence in the treatment of the figures and their dress

Great as these losses admittedly were, there were compensatory factors. The Arab occupation of the Byzantine provinces in the Levant had relieved the empire of troublesome districts which had developed separatist tendencies. Constantinople no longer had to worry about enforcement of unpopular ecclesiastical decisions in Syria and Egypt, nor about the political loyalty of the Monophysite populations. As the imperial boundaries receded, retrenchment produced a comparative strengthening of the state. This was due to the fact that the new borders corresponded more nearly with ethnic and religious lines, for the inhabitants of the empire were now largely Greek-speaking and Orthodox. Effective political control by Arabs, Slavs and Lombards had halted in eastern Anatolia, Thrace, Greece, southern Italy and Sicily, in just those areas where the Greek-speaking groups were strongest and resisted linguistic Arabization or Slavonization. The Islamic threat greatly subsided as a result of tribal strife which led to the overthrow of the Umayyads and the eastward transfer of the capital from Damascus to the regions of the Tigris–Euphrates.

These great territorial losses finally gave the Byzantine empire a cultural homogeneity which the reforms of Diocletian and Constantine and the magnificent achievements of Justinian had failed to produce. The effort to absorb the easternmost provinces had entailed greater assimilative powers than the empire could generate. Within the southern Balkans and Anatolia, however, Byzantine culture proved irresistible and by the sixth century the non-Greek languages of western and central Anatolia were dead or moribund. Lydian, Phrygian, Celtic, Lycian, Gothic, Cappadocian and Isaurian were first reduced to rural *patois* and finally extinguished before the language of administration, commerce and religion.

The large numbers of foreign groups which the emperors periodically settled in Anatolia similarly succumbed. The large settlement of Slavs in Greece caused the German historian Jacob Fallmereyer to remark that 'not a single drop of pure Greek blood flows in the veins of the modern Greeks'. A number of modern historians, under the influence of nineteenth-century racial theories which associated creative genius and cultural accomplishment with 'purity

54 The Great Mosque of Damascus (715), an example of Islamic adaptations of Byzantine culture

of blood', continue to accept his conclusions. However, the Mycenaean and classical Greeks were already products of ethnic mixture, so that even in antiquity the Greeks were not 'of pure blood', whatever that may mean. When the Slavic tribes came to Greece they settled in a society which was far more developed and so in the course of the centuries they were largely absorbed, Christianized, and Hellenized. In the Peloponnese they have left behind only their Slavic place-names and a few scattered notices in the sources as testimony to their former existence as a separate ethnic entity. Culturally, they seem to have had very little effect, a fact confirmed by the investigations of the Slavic philologist Miklosich who found only 129 words of Slav origin in the Greek language. In spite of the large number of Slavs who settled in Greece, investigation of the skeletons of ancient and modern Greeks has revealed a strong continuity in physical type. The physical anthropologist C. Coon was so struck by this evidence that he wrote in *The Races of Europe*:

It is inaccurate to say that the modern Greeks are different physically from the ancient Greeks; such a statement is based on an ignorance of the Greek ethnic character. In classical times the Greeks included many kinds of people living in different places, as they do today. If one refers to the inhabitants of Attica during the sixth century, or to the Spartans of Leonidas, then the changes in these localities have probably not been nearly as great as that between the Germans of Tacitus and the living South Germans, to cite but one example. . . . The Greeks, in short, are a blend of racial types. . . . The Nordic element is weak as it probably has been since the days of Homer. The racial type to which Socrates belonged is today the most important. . . . It is my personal reaction to the living Greeks that their continuity with their ancestors of the ancient world is remarkable rather than the opposite.

In the final analysis, however, it is the continuity of culture rather than physical type which is the critical factor, and the Slavs caused no break or alteration in this. The homogeneity which the empire now attained is reflected in the cultural transformation of the Armenians and Slavs who entered imperial service, as well as in the emergence of the new indigenous *theme* armies.

Byzantine society and economic life were undoubtedly affected by the loss of the urban centres of the Levant as well as by the violent destruction of city life by the Slavs in a large part of the Balkans. The complete disappearance of the towns in the empire would, of course, have meant the end of the Graeco-Roman traditions of Byzantine civilization. However, town life survived in the urban centres of Greece and Thrace where Sparta, Patras, Corinth, Athens, Thebes, Castoria, Thessalonica, Adrianople and Constantinople remained after the Slavic holocaust. But it was in Asia Minor that the Graeco-Roman towns remained, relatively speaking, shielded from ethnic migrations. Muslim and Christian caravans traversed the cities of the plateau, and merchant vessels visited the ports, so that the Anatolian towns served not only as administrative and ecclesiastical centres but also as focal points of commerce. The village clusters were closely bound to their metropolitan centres where the farmers went to sell their grain, buy goods, and to petition the patron saint at his shrine and the judge in his court. The provincial towns were connected with Constantinople by commercial as well as bureaucratic and religious bonds. The survival of this urban society was accompanied by a money economy to which government expenditure further contributed. Annual governmental disbursement in military pay for Anatolia may have reached 1,000,000 gold *solidi*, and the farmers paid part of their tax in gold. The urban and economic character of the empire thus differed from that of the west where manoralism had replaced urbanism.

The survival of Byzantium under such difficult conditions is not the sole evidence of its vitality, for by the middle of the ninth century the empire began to reimpose its culture upon most of those areas which the Slavs had taken. At this time the Moravian and Bulgarian princes requested the emperor to send missionaries who would introduce Christianity to their kingdoms. There ensued a bitter competition between Rome and Constantinople over Slav souls, and though Constantinople was forced to abandon Moravia, it succeeded in converting the Bulgars to the Byzantine version of Christianity. Cyril and Methodius, known as 'the apostles to the Slavs', laid the foundations of Orthodox Slavonic Christianity by creating a Slavonic alphabet for the translations of the liturgy and Scriptures from Greek into a Slav dialect. This was the beginning of a process which was to spread Byzantine culture to the south Slavs, Rumanians and Russians. The rôle of the Greek Church in Slav civilization parallels the rôle of the papacy in western Europe.

The Byzantine reconquista

The recovery from the crisis of the seventh century and the resultant consolidation in the eighth century produced a strengthened empire which was to attain new heights during the Macedonian dynasty (867–1056). Thanks to the patronage and guidance of the Macedonians the empire not only achieved spectacular military and social gains, but experienced a new literary and artistic flowering.

The initiative in these matters did not, it is true, come exclusively from the Macedonian dynasty, for Michael III and his advisers had already set out many of the directive lines which the Macedonians followed. In the two centuries after the accession of Basil I a new and glorious chapter was written in the pages of Byzantine military annals as the boundaries of the empire were expanded. The *reconquista* of the Macedonians was not as extensive as that of Justinian, but it had the virtue of being realistic. Warfare on the eastern frontier had become stabilized and by the ninth century had come to consist of raids and counter-raids, with the advantages often on the side of the Arabs. The development of this type of activity on the borders formed the *milieu* from which originated the medieval Greek epic, *Digenes Akritas*. Both in the epic and in the warfare against Islam one sees the existence and rise of the great military families of Anatolia, that is, the families of Phocas, Argyrus, Sclerus, Ducas, Maleinus and others. The power of these provincial dynasties developed from a combination of high positions in the army and extensive estates in the Anatolian districts.

The Byzantine advance on the eastern front began when Basil I decided to put an end to the border principality of the Paulicians. A dualist heretical sect of Armenian origin which rejected the Old and much of the New Testament, denied the efficacy of the Cross, relics and icons, abhorred developed ecclesiastical institutions, the Paulicians had succeeded with the aid of the Arabs in forming an independent state. After the sect had been uprooted in Byzantine territory by the empress Theodora, the Paulicians had fled to the Arabs and eventually established themselves in the city of Tephrike, whence they raided the Byzantine empire regularly. Their most capable leader was a former imperial official, Chrysocheir, who had hesitated between loyalty to the empire and defection to the heretics. The patriarch Photius had watched over Chrysocheir carefully, admonishing him to remain faithful, but Chrysocheir finally opted for a life of heresy and freebooting. His military campaigns were far more dangerous than those of his predecessors. They carried him as far west as Bithynia and Ephesus where he stabled his horse in the Church of St John (867–68), and his impudence was such that he

55 The Thessalonican brothers Cyril and Methodius, 'the apostles to the Slavs', are shown in this eleventh-century fresco kneeling before Christ in the presence of St Andrew, St Clement and angels

informed an imperial embassy which arrived in Tephrike in 869 that Basil should restrict himself to the European provinces and leave Anatolia to the Paulicians. One year later Basil managed to destroy a number of Paulician villages; but he suffered defeat before Tephrike and would have lost his life had it not been for the valour of an Armenian soldier, Theophylactus the Unbearable, father of the future emperor Romanus I Lecapenus. The event had a traumatic effect on Basil who thenceforth prayed daily in his chapel that he might not only live long enough to see Chrysocheir's death but also that he might personally pierce the heretic's skull with three arrows.

85

Two years later Chrysocheir was defeated and killed. The Paulicians fled eastward, Tephrike was occupied by the imperial armies, and a century later, when the advance of the imperial forces enabled them once more to establish contact with the Paulicians, John Tzimisces transplanted large numbers of them to Philippopolis, which from then on became the centre of these bellicose sectaries.

War against the Arabs would have followed the Paulician campaigns but for the involvement of the empire in Sicily, Italy and Bulgaria. The geographical location and extent of Byzantine possessions burdened the state with warfare on two very distant frontiers a thousand miles apart. In 904 the Arabs achieved their last great military success at the expense of Byzantium when the renegade Leo of Tripoli sacked Thessalonica and carried off into slavery 22,000 of its inhabitants.

With the accession of Romanus I Lecapenus, the offensive on the eastern front, which had lapsed with the end of the Paulician campaigns, was renewed. The architect of the new offensive in Anatolia was a Byzantine general of Armenian origin, John Curcuas, described in the sources as a second Belisarius and Trajan. His military talents and achievements inspired an eight-volume biography which unfortunately has not survived. Curcuas assumed direction of affairs in eastern Anatolia in 923 and for the next twenty years systematically pushed the Arabs back. His most significant victory was the recapture of the city of Melitene, which he Christianized by offering its Muslim inhabitants the choice of conversion or exile. More spectacular in the eyes of both Curcuas and his contemporaries was the return of the image of Christ on the silken towel which Christ is alleged to have sent to Abgar, the legendary king of Edessa. The Muslims of Edessa ransomed their city from the siege machines of Curcuas by giving him this celebrated image.

The momentum of the counter-offensive gathered strength under Nicephorus Phocas and John Tzimisces. Phocas, known as the 'white death of the Saracens', achieved the first of his spectacular victories with the reconquest of Crete in 960–61. Under the Arabs Crete had been a corsairs' lair whence the islands and shores of the Aegean were raided, and its possession had made possible the action on Thessalonica in 904. The reconquest was followed by the missionary activities of the Anatolian monk, St Nicon, who, after converting the Cretan Muslims, went on to Lacedaemonia to bring the faith to the unruly Slavs settled near Sparta. The expulsion of the Arabs from Crete and the occupation of Cyprus in 965 removed the danger of Arab naval raids on the Aegean and Anatolian coasts, and once more Byzantine naval power emerged as the decisive force in the eastern Mediterranean. In Anatolia Sayf ed-Daula made valiant efforts to avoid the final catastrophe which threatened the Hamdanid dynasty in Cilicia and northern Syria. But Aleppo, Sayf ed-Daula's capital, surrendered a year after the fall of Crete and he himself lived to hear the news of the fall of Tarsus in 965. When the imperial troops entered this important Cilician city they quickly transformed it into a Christian town by again offering the Muslims a choice between exile and conversion, and also by bringing in Greek and Armenian colonists.

The last great victory of Phocas' armies was the capture of Antioch in 969. The restoration of this patriarchal seat and commercial centre to the Christian empire after centuries of subjection to the infidel was the most stirring accomplishment of Phocas' reign. The religious passions of the combatants were the most salient features of the bitter struggle. For the Muslims the *jihad* or religious war was a duty enjoined by Islam. Phocas, highly religious and an ascetic, wished to have every soldier who fell in the wars declared a martyr for the faith, but was frustrated by the disagreement of the patriarch. Phocas' bellicosity is vividly revealed in a letter which he sent to the caliph in 964:

In the fighting in the passes your men of arms have been chased like a troop of animals. We have reduced to impotence your peasants and their women. The tall buildings have been destroyed and their ruins, once flourishing centres, have turned into an uninhabited desert. Only the owl's cry and its echo from the columns fill the solitude.

Antioch is not far . . . soon I shall reach it with a numerous multitude . . . O you who inhabit the deserts of sand, maledictions upon you. Return to your country of Sana, your first home. Soon I shall conquer Egypt by my sword and its richness shall swell my booty. . . .

I shall conquer all the east and west and I shall send out in all places the religion of the cross. Jesus has His throne which is elevated above all the heavens . . . while your prophet has been buried in the ground. May his bones decompose into dust . . . and his sons be plagued by death, captivity and dishonour.

The death of Phocas at the hands of the empress's lover John Tzimisces did not interrupt the war. Tzimisces completed the re-conquest in 975 by his triumphal procession through Syria, and the cities of Damascus, Sidon, and Beirut all capitulated to him. Once again in control of northern Syria, the emperors now turned to the Armenian and Georgian principalities of northeastern Anatolia. These were largely assimilated as a result of the policies of Basil II and his successors, so that by the mid-eleventh century Byzantine military might seemed all-powerful in the east.

56, 57, 58, 59 The religious significance of the imperial office was expressed in many ways. Leo VI, 'the Wise', kneels before Christ in a mosaic in Hagia Sophia (opposite). The ascetic Nicephorus Phocas (top) regarded his office as a crusading one and fought back the Arabs. John Tzimisces is crowned by the Virgin (above). Right, Constantine VII Porphyrogenitus, a great art-patron after the restoration of images, is crowned by Christ

The victories in the east had their parallels in the Balkans where the reign of Romanus I Lecapenus once again marks a turning-point. Earlier it had been far from evident that Byzantine arms would be successful for Symeon, who succeeded his father on the Bulgarian throne in 893, defeated and terrorized the empire until his death in 927. Not only did he force the imperial government to pay tribute, but when the emperor suspended the payments he advanced with his army to the walls of Constantinople itself. The weakness of the Byzantine government at that time was such that Symeon obtained the title of emperor, was crowned by the patriarch, and arranged the engagement of his daughter to the young Constantine VII. But the revolution which put Romanus Lecapenus in charge of affairs in Constantinople was a setback for Symeon, whose aim seems to have been to replace the Byzantine by a Bulgarian empire. The arrangements Symeon had made for his daughter's marriage, as well as his own coronation, were now cancelled and his frustration was completed when Romanus assumed the imperial title in 919 and arranged for the marriage of his own daughter to Constantine VII. Nevertheless, a compromise was reached five years later when Romanus met Symeon and accorded him the title of emperor, much as Michael I had done in the case of Charlemagne in 812, though it was made plain that it was not to apply to the Byzantine empire. Symeon then became involved with the Serbs and Croats, and when he died in 927 his son Peter, a more docile type, became an obedient son-in-law of Romanus I. Thenceforward Byzantine influence spread in the Bulgarian kingdom, though it was accompanied by the rise of the dualist heresy of the Bogomils.

In the reign of Phocas relations between Byzantium and Bulgaria once more became agitated and as the emperor was occupied with the Muslims he called on the Russian prince Svyatoslav for help. The latter defeated the Bulgarian armies on the banks of the Danube and by 969 had made himself master of the kingdom. This turn of events forced John Tzimisces to undertake the great expedition of 971 in which the Byzantine armies captured the Bulgarian capital of Great Preslav. Svyatoslav was forced to surrender at Silistria, and Tzimisces annexed Bulgaria and abolished the Bulgarian patriarchate.

Early in the reign of Basil II, however, the Bulgarians successfully revolted and formed a short-lived kingdom under the leadership of their tsar Samuel. Basil's efforts to subdue Samuel and prevent Bulgarian expansion were seriously impeded by wars with Islam, but even more by the revolt of the two most powerful Anatolian families in 986. For a moment it seemed as if the armies of Bardas Phocas and Bardas Sclerus would succeed in removing the Macedonian dynasty and in splitting the empire into a European and an Asiatic state. Eventually, however, Basil terminated the civil war successfully, but only after an exhausting struggle and with the support of Russian troops. He then put an end to Bulgarian resistance, crushing the enemy forces at the Struma River in 1014. Legend has it that he blinded 14,000 Bulgarian soldiers after the battle, and that when Samuel saw the dreadful sight he fell dead. Within a few years the entire Balkan peninsula was either in Byzantine hands or acknowledged imperial suzerainty.

The renewed power and self-confidence of the empire and its rulers produced a new collision with the western empire under Otto I. When Otto was crowned emperor in Rome in 962, his assumption of the imperial title was considered in Constantinople to be an usurpation, and his military expansions into southern Italy further agitated the Byzantine ruler. It was under these circumstances that Otto sent his emissary, Liudprand of Cremona, to Constantinople in order to arrange a marriage alliance and a dowry which would bring Byzantine Italian possessions to the Ottonians. Phocas' sense of imperial propriety was outraged no less than the sensibilities of Otto's ambassador, who has left an acerbic, yet witty, account of his embassy to Constantinople. Liudprand's account is something more, for it paints in bold strokes a picture of two societies which over the centuries have developed differently in every respect. Nicephorus Phocas repeatedly taunted Liudprand with the remark that his master was a king, not an emperor, and barbarian rather than a Roman, to which Liudprand variously replied that the title Roman was more appropriate to the inhabitants of Italy on the basis of language, or that the Romans as descendants of the slaves and murderers with whom Romulus founded Rome were inferior to the Lombards and

Saxons. His description of Phocas is an entertainingly vicious caricature:

He is a monstrosity of a man, a dwarf, fat-headed and with tiny mole's eyes; disfigured by a short, broad thick beard half going grey; disgraced by a neck scarcely an inch long; piglike by reason of the big close bristles on his head; in colour an Ethiopian and as the poet says, 'you would not like to meet him in the dark'.

Liudprand put forward the ancient Roman view of the Greeks, and quoted Virgil's opinion that 'their tongues are saucy, but cold are their hands in war'. Not only were the Greeks cowards but they were fond of flattery and given to greed and lying. Nicephorus, victorious over the Arabs, had equal scorn for western military and personal qualities, saying that the westerners were debilitated militarily because of the heaviness of their armour and weapons. The long hair and more elaborate robes of the Greeks, so different from western styles, Liudprand associated with Greek effeminacy, and his reaction to Greek cuisine was choleric. It was bad enough to live in draughty unheated halls, but to be expected to drink resinated wine and to eat dishes at imperial banquets which were heavily doused with vile fish sauces and garlic was insufferable. The vitriolic comments of Liudprand constitute an important commentary on the differences between the societies and cultures of east and west, and give a preview of the relations between Greeks and Latins as they emerged in the later period of Byzantine history.

Economic life
The fortunate political and military developments of the Macedonian period greatly fostered economic prosperity. The expansion of the frontiers brought new agricultural lands, manpower and revenues, and the cessation of Arab raids with the establishment of security allowed the rural population to cultivate their land in peace. The free peasant communities remained important sources of agricultural

60 Basil II, 'the Bulgar-slayer', under whom the Byzantine state reached its last great peak of power

οι τεωριοι

61, 62 The lives of ordinary men. Work in the vineyard (above)
and sheep-shearing, sailing, ploughing (opposite);
scenes from eleventh-century manuscripts

production alongside the estates of the great magnates. The technology of farming had probably changed little (in contrast to developments taking place in western Europe) since late antiquity, though
new crops such as rice and certain fruits had been introduced. The
methods of farming and the crops themselves remained remarkably
constant until the early modern period, and it is interesting that
this persistence of Byzantine agricultural traditions is still reflected
by the Greek loan-words in the spoken Turkish of Anatolia. The
main products of the rural areas were, of course, cereals, vegetables,
fruits, nuts, livestock, freshwater fish and timber. The river valleys
of western Asia Minor, the Pontic and southern coastal regions, and
Mesopotamia grew abundant wheat crops, whereas barley was the
principal grain in many of the plateau regions. In the Balkans the
centres of grain farming were Thrace and Thessaly. Greece and
Anatolia were then, as today, productive of a wide variety of fruits,
most of which were known in classical times though some (such as
the banana) seem to have been introduced into Anatolia in the
Byzantine period. The vineyards of Cappadocia were famous for
their wines in the Middle Ages, and Liudprand, as we have already
seen, commented upon the custom of putting resin in Greek wine,
a practice known in both classical and modern Greece.

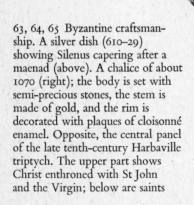

63, 64, 65 Byzantine craftsmanship. A silver dish (610–29)
showing Silenus capering after a
maenad (above). A chalice of about
1070 (right); the body is set with
semi-precious stones, the stem is
made of gold, and the rim is
decorated with plaques of cloisonné
enamel. Opposite, the central panel
of the late tenth-century Harbaville
triptych. The upper part shows
Christ enthroned with St John
and the Virgin; below are saints

Because of the survival of the Graeco-Roman urban centres the empire possessed a vast reservoir of craft skills which, when combined with the physical resources of the provinces, gave Byzantine industry the qualities of efficiency and excellence. Arab writers found the excellence of Byzantine craftsmen such that they could compare it only with the virtue of their Chinese equivalents; and a twelfth-century Latin author of a book on crafts included a number of technological processes of Byzantine origin. The regulative mentality of Byzantine statecraft intruded itself upon the organization of industry and was no doubt partly responsible for the high quality of the products, though regulation was used to control not only quality but also prices and the availability of goods.

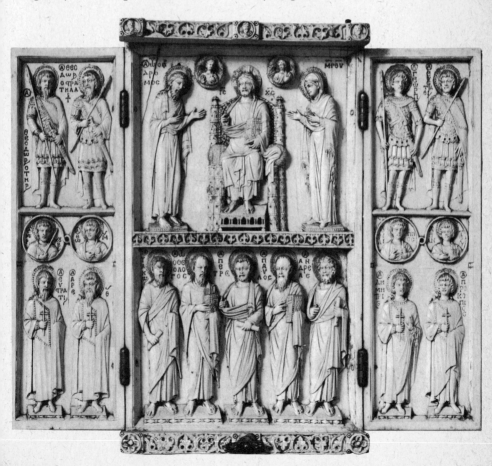

The state, through its urban officials, exercised supervision of the craftsmen via the corporations into which they were organized. The guilds, directly descended from those of the Graeco-Roman world, had a limited membership and many of their members managed to accumulate considerable wealth and achieved social prominence. By the later years of the Macedonian period the guilds were playing the same rôle as had the circus factions previously in the political life of the city, rioting and removing monarchs and unpopular officials. The most famous products of Byzantine industry were the luxury goods which the imperial goldsmiths and weavers created in the workshops of the palace. These brilliant textiles and jewels were reserved for the imperial family or for official gifts to foreign courts.

Industry seems to have been significant not only in Constantinople but in the provinces as well, where the raw materials were conveniently at hand. The mines of the Chalcidice, Euboea, Laurium and Anatolia yielded the essential metals, stone, and alum. The tradition of cloth-making was ancient in the urban centres of Greece, Asia Minor, and the Aegean isles; and in Byzantine times Corinth, Patras, Thebes, Laodicea, Cerasus, and Nicaea were famous for the products of their looms.

Constantinople under the Macedonians was the greatest emporium in the Christian world, and attracted merchants and goods from Europe, the Islamic lands, India, and China. It was also the economic centre of the empire, drawing upon the production of the provinces for the sustenance of its citizens and the armed forces. Each provincial city served as the economic focus of its neighbourhood where the villagers sold their agricultural produce and bought the products of the local craftsmen. The local fairs (*panegyreis*), usually associated with the local patron saint, attracted both Byzantine and foreign merchants. At the great fairs of Trebizond, merchants from the east sold perfumes and spices and bought Byzantine carpets and brocades. Since these merchants plied the Anatolian routes all the way to Constantinople, the provincial towns profited from international as well as local trade. The combination of territorial expansion and commercial prosperity produced so much state income that Basil II was able to remit taxes for a two-year period.

The rôle of the Church

In a society and period where religion and government were inseparable the expansion of the state's frontiers produced a corresponding expansion of the power of the Church. In all the reconquered provinces of the east, Orthodox bishops once more sat on the episcopal thrones from which the Orthodox clergy had previously been banished. The patriarchal see of Antioch experienced a revival of its pre-Islamic glory, but Byzantium had to face again the Monophysite problem. The Christians of northern Syria, the districts of Melitene and Armenia were predominantly Monophysite, and as the emperors attempted gradually to enforce ecclesiastical union, the Armenians and Syrians became increasingly restless in the eleventh century. Within the empire the increase of population and prosperity resulted in the creation of new bishoprics and metropolitan provinces. After the conversion of the Bulgars in the reign of Michael III Christianity and Byzantine culture spread throughout the Bulgarian kingdom in the ninth and tenth centuries. The Church demonstrated its vitality within the empire by its Christianization of the Slavs in the Peloponnese and Anatolia and the Muslims in Crete, an essential process without which provincial society could not have become unified.

The greatest victory of the Greek Church, however, was the conversion of Kievan Russia in the reign of Basil II. The emperor, having received substantial military reinforcements from Prince Vladimir to combat the serious rebellion of Bardas Phocas in Asia Minor, promised to give the Kievan prince his own sister Anna in marriage, provided that Vladimir and his people were converted to Christianity. The Russian aid was decisive in Basil's victory over the Anatolian rebels but the novelty of giving a daughter of the imperial house to a barbarian ruler was so distasteful that the emperor hesitated to fulfil his part of the agreement. When Vladimir attacked the Byzantine possessions in the Crimea, however, Basil gave way, with the result that Russia came under strong Byzantine influence at a time when the Russians were becoming civilized. The conversion of the Russians represents the greatest territorial expansion of Greek missionary activity, and Russian colonists were eventually to carry the Orthodox faith across Siberia to Alaska and California.

66, 67 Textile-workers were notable among Constantinople's craftsmen. This silk-weaving of the mid-eighth century (left) shows two riders hunting lions. Below, detail of a late tenth-century silk shroud

68 This eighth-century silk textile
portrays a lion strangler – Samson,
or possibly Hercules

The Iconoclastic controversy, which had been such a severe crisis
for the Church, stimulated a final burst of theological speculation on
the Christological issue, but thereafter the earlier theological vitality
of the Orthodox Church gave way to a concern for the preservation
of the faith in an unaltered form. Such further developments in
theology as there were could not compare with the earlier theological
accomplishments. On the other hand the monastic movement,
which had borne the brunt of the struggle with the Iconoclast
emperors, underwent a very intensive development and expansion
in the Macedonian period. Mysticism, intimately related to the
monastic life, remained an important element in Byzantine
religiosity. The appearance of the great mystic, Symeon the New
Theologian, symbolizes an intensification of personal religious
experience at a time when theological originality had disappeared.
Religious life became less intellectual and more emotional.

The traditional Byzantine sympathy and proclivity for the con-
templative life waxed stronger after the martyrdom which the
monks and nuns suffered at the hands of Constantine Copronymous
and his agents. Increasing numbers of men and women sought the
salvation of their souls in the monasteries which pious emperors,

69, 70 After the Iconoclast crisis monastic life increased in fervour, becoming more mystical and emotional, and less intellectual. The cell of a tenth-century monk can be seen (below) in this representation of St Luke from a Gospels. St Catherine's on Mt Sinai (right) survived the Islamic invasion of the Near East and North Africa, which caused a large-scale exodus of monks from the Levant

merchants, and peasants founded. The rapid increase in monastic foundations meant not only that large numbers of men withdrew from the affairs of the world, but that the monastic properties became a liability to the imperial fisc. Hence the emperors of the tenth and eleventh centuries resorted to legislation and confiscation in an effort to restrict the harmful effects of monastic growth. The Arab conquest of the Near East had caused a profound shift in the geographical centre of Byzantine monasticism as monks in great numbers fled from the Levant and re-established themselves in those lands still remaining in the empire.

The consequence was a decline in the importance of the eastern lands as monastic centres. The monasteries of Palestine, which had replaced the Egyptian monasteries in pre-eminence in the fifth and sixth centuries, still attracted some religious men but largely because the foundations were located in the Holy Land. The monasteries of northern Syria, closer to Christian lands and somewhat isolated from the Muslims by their mountainous situation, maintained a more lively existence, to which the Byzantine reconquest of this region gave a further stimulus. The most remarkable of the monasteries in Islamic lands was that of St Catherine's on Mount Sinai. Monks had settled around Mount Sinai as early as AD 400 and over two centuries later Justinian built the present church and the walls which surround it. Geographical isolation and Muslim protection explain the survival of the monastery's important collection of manuscripts and icons, but they render difficult any explanation of St Catherine's importance in the history of pilgrimage. Its location in Muslim lands fortunately removed the monastery from the Iconoclastic measures which destroyed the icons throughout the empire. Consequently, the monastery today possesses the only extensive collection of Byzantine painting, a collection which enables scholars to study the traditions of Byzantine painting from the pre-Iconoclastic period to modern times.

After the seventh-century Arab invasions Anatolia became the most important area of monastic activity (apart from Constantinople), and it remained so until the Seljuk invasions. Monastic foundations numbered hundreds, and Mount Olympus near Prusa and northwest Anatolia were populated by thousands of monks. The picture was the same throughout western Anatolia in the regions of Apamea, Ephesus, and Miletus. The most interesting physical remains of this vibrant monastic life are the conical troglodyte monasteries of Cappadocia some seventy miles southwest of Caesarea. Indicative of Anatolia's importance is the fact that St Athanasius, the real founder of Athonite monasticism, was a Trebizondine and that St Symeon the New Theologian was a Paphlagonian.

Constantinople had also become a very significant centre of monastic life since by the sixth century Egyptians, Syrians, Sicilians and Lycaonians had established religious houses for their compatriots in the city. The monastery of Studium had taken a commanding position under its abbot Theodore in the ninth century and his monastic rule exercised an important influence in the history of Byzantine monasticism. The vitality of this foundation is evident in the rôle which its abbots played in Church politics and in the importance of its scriptorium. The founding of new monasteries

71 The monastery of St Catherine's, built by Justinian, contains the only extensive collection of pre-Iconoclast Byzantine images, including this sixth-century Virgin enthroned

72 Interior of the rock-cut church of Tokale Kilise, Cappadocia, one of several built in the area after the Arab invasions

accelerated in the eleventh century and one modern scholar has been able (without any claim to completeness) to identify some three hundred monasteries in Byzantine Constantinople.

The principal event in the history of Greek monasticism during this era was the emergence of Mount Athos as a new monastic realm. Holy men had practised asceticism on the Holy Mountain as early as the ninth century. There was even an attempt to establish a coenobium in 870, but the growth of monasticism was hindered by the naval raids of the Muslim pirates of Crete. Only two years after Phocas' reconquest of Crete his friend Athanasius founded the Great Laura on Athos, and by the time Tzimisces issued the first document regulating life on the Mountain there were some fifty-eight settlements of monks. Within a century the number rose to 180, and this was further expanded by the appearance of large numbers of foreigners in the twelfth century. Russian monks appeared in the monastery of Xylourgou (1142), Savas founded a Serbian group at Chilandar (1198), the Georgian monastery of Iviron became prominent at an earlier date. Bulgars took over the Zographou

73 The church of St John of Studium, part of the great monastery in Constantinople that once played a vital part in Byzantine affairs

monastery, and the Christian descendant of a Seljuk sultan founded the house at Koutloumousiou in the twelfth century.

The growth of Mount Athos coincided with the decline of Turkish-dominated Anatolia and increasing Christianization of the Slavs. The monks of Mount Athos maintained a certain ecclesiastical independence from the patriarchs in Constantinople until the period of the Palaeologues, an autonomy which was observed by the Turks and is still in effect today. Indeed, Athos remained the spiritual focus of the whole of Orthodox monasticism until the early twentieth century. In its monasteries the monks cultivated and kept alive the mystical and ascetic traditions of the Byzantine fathers, copied and preserved their literary compositions, and of course continued the Byzantine style of painting. As late as the eighteenth century Russian, Rumanian, south Slav and Greek clergy were inspired by the Athonite community. The Russian cleric Velichkovsky, reacting to Latin influence in Russian seminaries, sought and found in the libraries of Athos the Byzantine sources of piety. These texts and the Painter's Manual were translated from the Greek into the various languages of the Orthodox faithful with the result that Byzantine traditions of spirituality and art were temporarily renewed.

Of the monasteries in Greece and the Aegean islands the churches of Hosius Lucas (Phocis), Daphni, and Nea Mone (Chios) are well known for their exquisite mosaics, and the monastery of St John on Patmos (late eleventh century) for its manuscripts. The Greek monastic foundations in Sicily and southern Italy, however, were more remarkable. Their development apparently coincided with the settlement of monks who fled from the Arabs in the seventh century, and in a manner resembles the experience of Anatolian monasticism. These establishments, of which there were hundreds, developed their own hagiography and art, and helped to spread Byzantine civilization in the region. The most famous of these monasteries, inspired by St Neilus (d. 1004), was Grottaferrata, but other Greek monasteries existed as far north as Rome.

Though monasticism had obvious social defects and was intellectually obscurantist, it also had its meritorious side, for monasteries often provided charity and education to the Christians. The *typika*, which regulated the life of the monks in the various houses, often record that sums of money were set aside for the care of the poor, orphans, the sick, travellers, etc. Similarly, they describe the contents of the monastic library which were largely, though not exclusively, of a religious nature. The monks in the scriptoria were perennially busy copying manuscripts, and it is thought by some that the scribes of Studium were responsible for introducing a large-scale reform of Byzantine script in the ninth century. This conservative rôle of the monks in preserving literature was essential for Byzantine education and is responsible for having saved much of Byzantine writing from oblivion.

Just as their spiritual needs necessitated the copying of manuscripts, the demands of worship stimulated the development of painting in the monasteries. Probably the basic significance of monasticism was that it fulfilled the desire of the Byzantine Christian to abandon the world and seek the salvation of his soul in the community of holy men. It has been suggested that the flight of men to the monasteries was often motivated by base considerations, but this alone would not

74 Christ Pantocrator, ruler and stern judge. Dome mosaic at Daphni, near Athens, *c.* 1100

account for the great spread of monastic life throughout the empire. Mysticism, which received a further elaboration in the writings and life of Symeon the New Theologian, represents a refinement of the procedure by which the pious could attain salvation.

The Macedonian contribution to Byzantine culture

The Macedonian period constituted a kind of renaissance, marked by a significant increase in literary output, educational activity and a return to the classical authors. It is true that interest in pagan literature had never completely disappeared, but from the ninth century until the end of the empire scholars had increasingly intimate contact with this body of material. The new trends were in part the result of imperial patronage and the intellectual interests of certain exceptional individuals, but the return to ancient tradition was reflected in other fields and literary classicism was only part of a broader archaistic current. Side by side with the classical revival in literature and education in the Macedonian era, the traditional religious modes continued in both fields, usually through the efforts of the monks.

The history of the university founded in Constantinople during the fifth century is obscure, but it was refounded in the ninth century by the caesar Bardas, who appointed Leo the Philosopher as its head. The revival of intellectual interests in Byzantine court circles coincides with the great translations of Greek works into Arabic at the court of Mamun in Baghdad, and one historical anecdote has it that the promotion of Leo, first to the archbishopric of Thessalonica and then to the directorship of the university, was prompted by an offer of the caliph for the services of this learned man. A contemporary remarked that the emperor Theophilus regarded science 'as if it were a secret to be guarded, like the manufacture of Greek fire, deeming it bad policy to enlighten barbarians.'

75 In the arts the Iconoclast controversy resulted in an upsurge of classicism, apparent in this illumination from the tenth-century *Theriaca* of Nicandor

76 The ivory carving on the Veroli Casket (tenth-eleventh centuries) is consciously classical in subject and treatment, though Europa riding her bull is oddly set in a scene of violent stoning

111

The tenth century is dominated by the figure of Constantine VII Porphyrogenitus, who not only patronized but also actively participated in the scholarly activity of the day. The circle which he formed at court was responsible for a large number of works, generally in the form of compilations, which were intended mainly to preserve useful information. The emperor himself composed a manual *On the Administration of the Empire*, as a diplomatic handbook for his son so that he might know how to deal with the various foreign nations. Similarly his treatise *On the Ceremonies of the Byzantine Court* was written in order to preserve the elaborate court ceremonial, and thus contribute to the power and glory of the empire. Members of the imperial circle also wrote histories intended to fill gaps in the accounts of the empire's affairs, while other encyclopædic works of the tenth century included the *Lexicon of Suidas*, the *Lives of the Saints* written by Symeon Metaphrastes, and an earlier collection of epigrams known to classical scholars as the *Anthologia Palatina*. They are important as historical sources and as evidence of scholarly and literary continuity on a relatively sophisticated level.

After the death of Constantine and his son Romanus, men of an entirely different temper ascended the throne. Nicephorus Phocas and John Tzimisces were the scions of great landowning families in the provinces of Anatolia, little given to intellectual pursuits but devoted to bellicose undertakings against the empire's foes. They sought diversion and edification not from men steeped in the classical literary culture but rather from the monastic ascetics who were the intellectual descendants of St Anthony and St Pachomius. Basil II, defending his position against rough soldiers of this type, adopted their attitude, with the result that there was a century-long hiatus in imperial support for education and the intellectuals. Secular education continued, however, on a private, individual level and it was sufficient to produce one of the greatest polymaths of the entire Middle Ages, Michael Psellus.

The bureaucratic interlude of the eleventh century, which followed the death of Basil II (1025), increased the government's need for well-educated officials. In part because of this need, in part as a consequence of the rise of three intellectuals (Psellus, Xiphilinus,

Leichudes) to prominence in the bureaucracy, and in part because of the personality of Constantine IX the university was reopened in 1045. Its primary duty was to turn out well-educated officials for the bureaucracy, rather like the classical examination system by which the Chinese civil service was recruited. The constitution of the law school in the University of Constantinople specifically stated that no student could practice law until he had finished the courses and received written and oral testimony to his competence from the professors. Unfortunately, the constitution of the second of the two faculties, philosophy, has not survived, but something is known of its character. The director (with the title 'consul of the philosophers') was Psellus: thus direction of the university was completely in the hands of the bureaucrats, for Xiphilinus was head of the law school. In the philosophical school the candidates first studied grammar, then rhetoric under Nicetas and John Mauropus, and terminated their studies with philosophy under Psellus. Psellus, with his characteristic lack of modesty, remarked at the height of his career, that Celts, Arabs, Persians and Ethiopians came to Constantinople to hear his lectures. He was responsible for the revival of interest in Plato's writings which thenceforward remained an important feature of Byzantine scholarly life. A prolific author, his writings, both prose and poetry, range over the whole spectrum of Byzantine literature: a history of the eleventh century, a rich letter-collection encompassing all the important individuals in the society of his day, philosophical excurses, encomia, condemnations, commentaries (on law, science, magic, proverbs), and even a topography of classical Attica. Though Psellus, Xiphilinus, and Mauropus fell out of favour with Constantine IX and the university may have suffered a temporary setback, it soon recovered for by the latter half of the eleventh century John Italus is found teaching Plato and Aristotle at the university as 'consul of the philosophers'.

Secular education based on the study of the pagan classics emerges as a vital force in the intellectual formation of Byzantine society. Psellus, while still a boy, could recite the entire *Iliad* by heart, and a knowledge of Homer was sufficiently widespread for the man in the street to describe the beauty of Constantine Monomachus' mistress

78 Plaques from the crown of Constantine IX Monomachus (1042–55) with portraits of the empress Zoe, Constantine himself and Zoe's sister, Theodora

in verses from his poetry. However, there was a polarization of Byzantine education and literature between a classical and a religious orientation. The appearance of a Psellus was balanced by the life of his monastic counterpart, Symeon the New Theologian. Psellus considered philosophy to be more than a mere auxiliary to theology. It was the mistress of all knowledge, whereas theology was merely one branch of knowledge. Symeon, though a highly intelligent man, avoided pagan literature in the course of his education (a point on which his biographer lays great stress) and emphasized the importance of man's emotional experience rather than the exercise of the rational faculties. For the pious monks the study of the Church Fathers and the lives of the saints were the proper models for the formation of the mind. This difference in outlook led to an attack on Leo the Philosopher's secular curriculum in the university during the

79 The Hellenistic influence in secular art. David composing the Psalms, from the ninth-century Paris Psalter

ninth century and it finally caused Xiphilinus (after he became patriarch) to attack Psellus' attachment to philosophy. Thus the ambivalence of the Byzantine mind towards the classical heritage remained a characteristic of Byzantine life, which, in spite of the synthesis of the Cappadocians, never disappeared.

The prosperity and patronage of the Macedonians served as a powerful stimulus to Byzantine artists, who created a second golden

80 The monastic reaction against secular Hellenism. Paradise and the Four Rivers, from the twelfth-century Homilies of Jacob of Kokinobaphos

age in Byzantine art. Developments in art and literature were amazingly parallel for both were characterized by a rediscovery of and inspiration by ancient models, and by the tension between secular taste and religious sensitivity. Though Iconoclasm had imposed restrictions on religious artistic expression, it had opened the way for a return to Alexandrian traditions, and Byzantine art consequently turned to profane-historical themes and borrowed pure ornamentation

117

from the Arab east. The taste of the Macedonian rulers gave rise to an imperial art which was strongly influenced by ancient models and was largely secular. When Basil I built the new palace (*Kainourgion*) its chambers were decorated with mosaics depicting the emperor enthroned and surrounded by his victorious generals presenting him with cities which they had reconquered. There were also vignettes depicting the emperor's personal deeds of valour, and the emperor's bedchamber contained mosaics of Basil and his empress enthroned, and of floral decoration.

This imperial style extended to the affluent aristocrats who apparently decorated their mansions in a similar manner. The description of the palace of the epic hero Digenes Akritas is no doubt typical. The poet describes paintings depicting the deeds of Achilles and Bellerophon, the defeat of Darius, and the victories of Alexander. Mythological and profane scenes are prominent on the ivories of the eleventh century, and the illuminations in manuscripts of such pagan authors as Nicander, Oppian and Apollonius are further indications of this secular trend.

Works of art in churches and monasteries gave expression to an opposed tendency at a time when monasticism was undergoing a phenomenal expansion. The ecumenical council of 787 had subjected religious art in churches to dogmatic considerations with the result that such art developed a powerful iconographic tradition in the Macedonian epoch. Nevertheless, the return to ancient modes was such a strong impetus that imperial art had a corresponding influence on religious art. This influence is most evident in the miniatures of religious manuscripts in which the miniaturist often borrows from ancient themes, mythological scenes and allegories. There is a striving for realism through the employment of the picturesque and a reliance upon architectural and landscape details. But by the twelfth century the theological tendency of the monastic element succeeded in subduing the profane and classical tendency in religious art. A comparison of the ninth-century Paris Psalter with the twelfth-century manuscript of the Homilies of the monk Jacob of Kokinobaphos illustrates very clearly the rejection of the secular by the religious. In the Paris Psalter, David is presented in such a manner as to recall Orpheus, surrounded by landscapes, architecture, animals, plants and personifications, all of which are Hellenistic. In the twelfth-century manuscript the artist has turned his back on the ancient models and has reverted to a more theological treatment.

There is nothing surprising about the strength of the religio-monastic element in Byzantine literary and artistic traditions, for the same was the case in western Europe. The remarkable thing is that the classical tradition remained so strong. Though this rich classical heritage may have had a stifling effect on literary creativity, its effects in the field of art were more positive, and here the work it inspired was truly original. In any event, the classical inheritance was the basis of Byzantine superiority over the contemporary west in literary and artistic standards.

81 Romanus II and Eudoxia crowned by Christ; an ivory relief of the mid-tenth century

119

82 The emperor Nicephorus III Botaniates (1078–81) between St John Chrysostom and the Archangel Michael

On the death of Basil II (1025) the power and glory of Byzantium seemed to be securely established, for not since the Heraclian reconquests had the empire experienced a comparable expansion. The state's boundaries stretched from the Danube to Crete and from southern Italy to Syria. The eastern waters had once more become a Byzantine lake where the Greek fleets cruised about freely from their advance bases in Crete and Cyprus. The brilliant victories of the late tenth and early eleventh centuries had brought peace to the empire, and greatly contributed to the cultural flowering of the eleventh century. The conversion of Russia had resulted in a parallel expansion of the Church, making it a formidable rival of the papacy. The great conquests had increased the wealth of the state, filling its treasury to overflowing. Because of the growth in revenues and the new booty Basil II had to build extensive underground vaults so that the treasury could accommodate this vast income. The peace and affluence which followed the death of Basil served as a powerful stimulus to art and literature both in the capital and the provinces. The activity of Psellus and his circle in Constantinople coincided with great architectural activity in the provinces.

INTERNAL PROBLEMS

Yet, within half a century of Basil's death, both the Macedonian dynasty and the prosperity which it had created had disappeared. In the early years of the reign of Alexius I Comnenus (1081–1118) the empire had declined to a pale shadow of its former glory, its possessions largely contained by Adrianople in the west and the Bosphorus in the east. So complete was this decline that it is quite startling to the historian. Its cause was a remarkable confluence of internal ills which exhausted the body of the empire as it was being attacked from the outside by vigorous new forces. The most virulent of these illnesses was the strife between the civil bureaucrats and the provincial generals.

Since the very foundation of the empire by Diocletian and Constantine there had existed a sharp division between the men of the pen and those of the sword, a tension noticeable in other highly-developed empires, such as the Chinese and Islamic. The separation of civil and military power by Diocletian had tended to weaken the military class, but with the system of *themes*, and the subordination of both powers to the generals, the military class again became powerful. Their domination of society was further facilitated by the fusion of the *strategoi* with the great provincial landowners. The successes of Byzantine arms in the tenth and eleventh centuries bred a great arrogance in this military class and an ambition to overthrow the hegemony of the bureaucrats within the government. Thanks to his cruel vigour Basil II was able to bridle these ambitions through military action and unrelenting persecution; and the sequestered lands of the magnates constituted an important source of revenue for the imperial fisc under him. But Basil was succeeded by his incompetent brother Constantine, and when Constantine died, leaving three daughters as heirs, the lack of a competent male successor, who could control the military and their competition with the bureaucracy, brought disaster.

At first the bureaucratic circle of the capital, consisting among others of eunuchs, university professors and the aristocratic families of Constantinople, established its control over the organs of government and successfully frustrated the ambitions of the generals. The difference in character of the two groups manifested itself in rebellions of the generals and retaliatory persecutions by the civil officials. Upon the death of Constantine VIII the succession devolved upon his unmarried daughter Zoe, and the competition of the bureaucrats and soldiers centred about the choice of the empress's husband. Though the legal fiction of dynastic succession was maintained, it was grotesquely perverted by the plots of the two factions contending to furnish their own candidates as prince-consort. Until 1057 the generals were repeatedly defeated, unleashing in the course of this thirty-years period at least one major rebellion annually.

So long as representatives of the dynasty survived, the bureaucrats were successful in maintaining their hegemony, for dynastic sentiment had taken firm root in the people of Constantinople. This was manifested clearly when Michael V unsuccessfully attempted to put an end to the Macedonian line. The nephew of an obscure eunuch, John Orphonotrophus, who had succeeded where the powerful generals had failed (by promoting successive love-affairs between Zoe and his nephews), Michael V dared to banish Zoe from the palace. The wrath of the Constantinople guildsmen and citizens put a violent end to his attempted usurpation. The power which possession of the capital gave the administrative officials was dramatically stated by the general Cecaumenus, who advised his son never to rebel against the emperor since whoever possessed Constantinople would always prevail.

VICTORY OF THE MILITARY

The first success of the generals took place in 1057 in the rising of Isaac Comnenus. It is significant that the principal Anatolian aristocrats joined the ranks of the revolutionaries in Asia Minor, but in spite of this formidable array the civil element might have remained secure in Constantinople had it not been for certain significant developments within the city. There the leader of the civil aristocracy, Constantine Ducas, had become dissatisfied with the control which the court eunuchs and officials exercised over Michael VI. Consequently he joined the conspiracy of Comnenus and, as he was married to the niece of the patriarch Cerularius, this no doubt helped to swing Cerularius to the side of the Anatolians. Psellus, head of the senate and the intellectuals in the bureaucracy, had been closely associated with Ducas in former years; hence it is no surprise that he betrayed Michael VI to the advancing armies. When Isaac Comnenus approached Constantinople the patriarch unleashed a rebellion of the guildsmen which culminated in the removal of Michael VI and the accession of a general to the throne. Isaac I could boast that he had taken the empire with the sword (he did so by depicting himself with sword in hand on the gold coinage), but the victory of the military was a hollow one inasmuch as the assistance of the bureaucratic leader Constantine Ducas had made it possible. When Isaac retired from the throne (1059) Ducas succeeded him and the bureaucrats under the direction of Psellus pursued the military establishment relentlessly. Until the final victory of the military aristocracy under Alexius I (1081) the course of the struggle vacillated between the two sides.

The prolonged struggle between the generals and civil officials convulsed the empire at a critical period. The generals, frustrated by the officials in the capital, had recourse to the armies which they commanded and repeatedly denuded the frontiers of military forces in order to attack their enemies in the capital. They did this at a time when the pressure of the Seljuks, Patzinaks and Normans was increasingly threatening the frontiers of the empire. The employment of the armies in the political struggle not only diminished their numbers and effectiveness, but finally led to the systematic disbanding of the native levies by the bureaucrats who had every reason to fear them. The military service of the inhabitants in the border regions was commuted to a cash payment, and funds were generally withheld from the military so that by the time of Constantine X Ducas the bureaucrats had effectively destroyed the national armies and replaced them with mercenary Normans, Germans, Patzinaks and Armenians.

124

83 Coin of Isaac Comnenus, sword in hand – indicating that the imperial crown was his by right of the sword

This return to mercenary armies was a serious weakness which played a significant rôle in the collapse of the state. The loyalty of the mercenaries extended only as far as their cash subsidy, but the empire fell on hard times and more often than not the subsidies were not forthcoming. The foreign troops then began to victimize the empire they had been hired to protect, plundering the inhabitants and in some cases attempting to carve out states of their own. The hostility between the bureaucrats and soldiers found expression in the literature of the times. Cecaumenus, a rough, wily soldier who wrote in the vernacular rather than the cultivated language of a Psellus, admonished his son: 'Do not wish to be a bureaucrat, for it is not possible to be both a general and a comedian.' Another chronicler, writing of the reign of Michael VII and his teacher Psellus, was equally sarcastic:

85 Students and teachers; illumination from the fourteenth-century Skylitzes Codex

[Michael Ducas] busied himself continuously with the useless and unending study of eloquence and with the composition of iambics and anapaests; moreover he was not proficient in this art, but being deceived and beguiled by the consul of the philosophers [Psellus], he destroyed the whole world.

The imbalance between sword and pen ranks foremost among the causes which led to the collapse of the Byzantine empire.

SOCIAL AND ECONOMIC CHANGES

Side by side with this rise of the generals there was a certain 'feudalizing' of the empire's society, for the generals were simultaneously owners of vast landed estates with large armed retinues of their own. The fusion of the landed magnate with the *strategos* was complete by the early tenth century and the generalship of an Anatolian province became virtually hereditary in families such as those of Sclerus, Phocas and Argyrus. The expansion of these families' land-holdings and the growth of population in the provinces created a great land hunger in the tenth century which endangered the free communities of peasant land-holders. Though Byzantium's economy was based on a cash currency and men often became wealthy in shipping and industry, the principal form of investing capital was the purchase of land. In the case of the aristocrats this propensity for acquiring land was further stimulated by the fact that the government had excluded the upper classes from many business enterprises.

As the expansion of this class threatened to devour the free peasants the emperors issued a series of vigorous laws which attempted to halt this process and to stabilize agrarian relations between the two classes. Romanus I Lecapenus, who promulgated the first of these decrees, realized that the disappearance of the free villagers would undermine the entire fiscal, military and social foundations of the empire. He and succeeding emperors ordered the return of the land to the peasants, but the very frequency of these laws is clear proof of their ineffectiveness. It could not have been otherwise, for their implementation was often in the hands of the very class against which they were directed. The danger which such a landed aristocracy presented was made abundantly clear in the rebellion of Phocas and Sclerus against Basil II. The size of the magnates' possessions was so enormous that Eustathius Maleinus, for example, could entertain Basil II with his army for an extended period of time.

Upon the death of Basil the last restraint on the magnates vanished and in the course of the eleventh century they effectively (though not completely) eliminated the free peasantry. It was upon the magnates that the general-emperor Alexius Comnenus, who succeeded in 1081, based his government. The result was that the army passed under aristocratic control. Already in the mid-eleventh century the emperors had begun to grant state properties in usufruct to those who had performed important services to the state. Such grants, known as *pronoia*, became the basis of military service under Alexius. The transformation of the *pronoia* into something comparable to the western fief created a military landowning society in Byzantium which differed from that of the Latin west only in that the elements of homage and sub-infeudation were missing. It is true that the emperors retained control over the *pronoia* system for a long time. But eventually it became decentralized, and when the Latins conquered the empire in 1204 the Greek aristocracy in many places recognized in the Latin barons and fiefs the counterparts of the Byzantine *archontes* and *pronoiai*.

The Macedonian expansion had once more brought large ethnic groups within the empire's borders without being able to absorb them culturally. Basil's conquest of Bulgaria had culminated in the

86 Armenian architecture. The cathedral of Ani, designed by an identified Armenian architect, Trdat, was built between 989 and 1001

subjugation of the land, but even so there were a few rebellions on
the part of the Bulgarians during the eleventh century. Further south
there was an unsuccessful rising among the Vlachs in Thessaly during
the reign of Constantine X, though this does not seem to have been
motivated by ethnic considerations. More serious, however, were
the ethnic problems which the emperors encountered in eastern
Anatolia, for large numbers of Armenians and Syrians inhabited the
regions which the Macedonian dynasty conquered. Moreover,
the emperors colonized those areas which the Muslims vacated, such
as Melitene and Cilicia, with Armenians and Syrians as well as
Greeks. In the eleventh century the Turkish raids also drove large
numbers of Armenians into Byzantine territory with the result that
a large Armenian element settled in Cappadocia side by side with
the Greeks.

The presence of these new elements raised problems for the state not only because the Armenians retained their political and military institutions, forming a state within a state but also because both the Armenians and Syrians were Monophysites. The principal measure by which the empire attempted to absorb these new elements was ecclesiastical union, a policy which had failed to integrate the non-Greek elements of the east in the sixth and seventh centuries and which now failed again with tragic results. The main effort to bring about union took place in the reign of Constantine X Ducas (1059–67). First the Syrians were summoned to Constantinople, but when their ecclesiastical leaders refused to agree to union they were exiled. In 1065 it was the turn of the Armenian clergy and princes. Though for a moment it seemed as if the negotiations would succeed, in the end Kakig Bagratouni, the former king of Ani, refused to give his consent. But although the Armenians, in contrast to the Syrians, were allowed to return to eastern Anatolia, Kakig declared war on the Greek clergy and population and slew the archbishop of Caesarea. It was his intention to desert to the Turks, but he was slain by the Greeks before he could do so.

87 Armenian art. Eleventh-century miniature showing the Holy Women at the Sepulchre

A few years later the Greeks of Sebasteia complained to Romanus IV that they had suffered more from the Armenians than from the Turks, and the emperor had to exercise great caution in these areas lest they should attack his armies. The old Monophysite problem emerged once more, as it had in the seventh century, to threaten the security of the empire. The council of 1605 which so exacerbated relations between Monophysites and the Orthodox had a much more immediate and important effect upon the political fate of Byzantium than did the schism of 1054 between Greeks and Latins. The former played a critical part in the Turkish conquest of Anatolia; the latter became important only in the twelfth century and then partly as a result of the loss of Anatolia.

A growing economic illness, the basic cause of which are not clear, greatly complicated the empire's difficulties. To what degree the growth of monastic and private estates reduced state revenues in the eleventh century it is difficult to say, but doubtless it played a growing rôle. There seems to have been considerable mismanagement of state finance after the death of Basil II due to the prodigality of emperors and empresses while the growth of the mercenary units in the army further strained the imperial purse. But perhaps the most serious decline in revenues arose as the Patzinaks and Seljuks raided the provinces and rendered them unproductive. If the causes of the economic decline are not clear their manifestation in the coinage is evident enough. From its institution by Constantine I until the early eleventh century the Byzantine gold *solidus* had undergone very little change, remaining stable for seven hundred years. In the first half of the eleventh century it suffered a growing debasement until by 1080 it contained only a very small percentage of gold. In a centralized state which relied upon money to support its military and bureaucratic structures the financial collapse was of course very serious.

THE EXTERNAL THREAT

As these developments undermined the empire, new peoples appeared on the far-flung borders and advanced while the empire progressively weakened. Basil II had contemplated the reconquest of Sicily from the Arabs, but he did not live long enough to carry out his plans. The victorious campaigns of George Maniaces, which temporarily brought Syracuse and eastern Sicily under Byzantine authority, might ultimately have succeeded had the persecution of the military by the bureaucracy in Constantinople not caused Maniaces to rebel in 1043. This Byzantine general had, significantly, employed Norman mercenaries during his Sicilian campaigns. Sixteen years later the Norman adventurers, under the leadership of Robert Guiscard, began to establish themselves as an independent power in the Byzantine lands of southern Italy. The political instincts of the Scandinavians, who had already intervened in Russia, France and England, made the Normans the most dangerous of all mercenaries and by the latter half of the century they threatened the Byzantine empire from within and without.

In the north the nomadic peoples of the Altai once more cast their shadow upon the Balkan provinces for the Patzinaks, a Turkic people who had played an important part in Byzantine diplomacy, crossed the Danube in 1048 and began to raid the empire. Constantine Monomachus eventually gave them lands in the Balkans where they were to exercise the function of border troops, and much to the disgust of the bureaucrats he raised the Patzinak chieftains to the rank of senators. The disturbances which they caused greatly increased when another Turkic people, the Uzes, invaded the Balkans as they sought to flee from the Cumans. Their depredations spread death and destruction so widely that the inhabitants seriously thought of evacuating the Balkan peninsula.

The most important of these nomadic peoples were the Seljuk Turks who began to plunder Anatolia in the first half of the eleventh century. The Seljuks, so named after an eponymous ancestor, were descended from the Oguz Turks who had established a great empire in Mongolia during the sixth, seventh and eighth centuries. After the break-up of this state various Turkic tribes moved westwards along the Russian steppe to the Balkans, or south of the Caspian to the borders of the Islamic world. The Patzinaks and Uzes are representatives of the Turkic peoples who followed the more northerly route, the Seljuks of those who followed the route to the Muslim lands. Converted to Islam in the tenth century, the Seljuks entered the eastern lands of the Islamic peoples as the mercenaries of warring states. Under the leadership of Toghril they established a great kingdom in Persia and revived the caliphate at a time when it was very weak. The power of the Seljuk sultans derived from their nomadic Turkish tribes, but once the sultans had established themselves as the rulers of much of the Middle East the recalcitrant tribesmen were too difficult to control. Therefore they were shunted to the borders of the Byzantine empire where their bellicose nature and desire for booty could be satisfied at the expense of the Christian foe. Muslim authors bear ample testimony to the fear which those nomads inspired in the sedentary society of Islam, one Persian official even advising that the thumbs of the Turks should be hacked off so that the nomadic horsemen might not draw their dreaded bows.

THE CRISIS OF 1071

In 1071 the deteriorating internal and external conditions very nearly destroyed the empire. This was the year when Bari, the last Byzantine possession in Italy, was lost, thus ending the centuries of Byzantine domination in southern Italy, while at the other end of the empire the Seljuks defeated Romanus IV at the battle of Manzikert and began the conquest and settlement of Anatolia. This process, which was to last four hundred years, marks one of the great turning points of world history, since it was the basic factor in the transition from the Byzantine to the Ottoman empire. Romanus IV (1067–71), a representative of the Anatolian generals, had successfully plotted to gain the throne with the intention of rescuing the empire from the wretched state to which Constantine Ducas had brought it. His vigorous military expeditions against the Turks in Anatolia were the last glimmer of the warrior traditions of Basil II, but Romanus was too late. The armies which served him were composed largely of unreliable mercenaries, and the plots of Psellus with the Ducas family effectively frustrated his undertakings.

When in 1071 Romanus set out for his third Anatolian campaign, the progress of his journey was marred by ill omens at every stage.

88 A Byzantine army defeated by the Turks;
miniature from the Skylitzes Codex

First the imperial tent collapsed; then a fire consumed the royal
stables; the Greeks of Sebasteia complained to him of Armenian
treachery; on another occasion his foreign mercenaries attacked him;
and finally his forces marched past a battlefield cn which lay the
bleached bones of a previously defeated Byzantine army. Romanus
divided his forces into three groups, with one of which he encamped
by the city of Manzikert in the vicinity of which, unknown to the
emperor, were the forces of the Seljuk sultan, Kilij Arslan. The battle
which ensued was a military accident. Neither ruler was aware of
the presence of the other, and Romanus had fatally divided his forces.
Even after the scouts on both sides had informed their rulers of the
situation the battle could have been avoided, for Kilij Arslan asked
the emperor for peace. Romanus, however, decided that he must
settle the Turkish issue once and for all, for the Turks were elusive
and it was hard to come to grips with them.

The events of the battle reflect only too accurately the evils which
plagued the empire. The Armenian soldiers, as a result of religious
animosity, deserted *en masse* on the field of battle, as did a small body
of Patzinaks. But the most important factor in the Byzantine defeat
was the premeditated desertion of the general Andronicus Ducas,
nephew of Constantine X Ducas and a leading personality in the
bureaucratic faction. He had decided to secure the future of his
family (Romanus had exiled his father) and as commander of the
rear-guard he spread the false rumour that the emperor had been
defeated, and retired from the battle with his forces. His withdrawal

133

spread panic throughout the Byzantine army, and the emperor was taken captive and brought before the joyous sultan who treated him with honour.

Adronicus returned to Constantinople with news of the defeat and the bureaucratic faction proceeded to the coronation of Michael VII Ducas. Kilij Arslan had in the meantime released Romanus and the existence of two rival emperors plunged the empire into civil war just at the moment when Turkmen tribes began to enter Anatolia unopposed. During the next ten years the quarrelling bureaucrats and generals bid against each other for the services of the Turkmen chieftains in the civil strife, handing many towns over to Turkish garrisons and ensuring the success of the Turkish occupation. The loss of Anatolia to the Turks was to prove fatal to the empire, for without its rich provinces Constantinople remained a huge head deprived of the body needed to sustain it.

REVIVAL UNDER ALEXIUS I COMNENUS

When Alexius Comnenus ascended the throne he possessed an empire reduced to such pitiful straits that its days seemed numbered. That the empire was saved and its life prolonged another three and a half centuries is a remarkable testimony to the qualities of this soldier-emperor. The Comnenoi not only saved the empire, bringing it a last glimmer of greatness, but they managed to do this with resources which were marginal at best, for Anatolia was largely lost to the Turks. No sooner had Alexius donned the imperial purple than he was faced by a Norman invasion which could easily have delivered the knock-out blow. By now Robert Guiscard had consolidated his hold on southern Italy, and decided to conquer Constantinople, for the Normans had undergone a certain measure of Byzantinization following their conquest of the former Byzantine province. The Norman rulers eventually adopted the Byzantine autocratic style in their architecture, representation on coins, etc. Meanwhile, Norman society in southern Italy was remarkably rich, drawing on Greek, Lombard and Arab elements. The Norman chancellery and coinage were trilingual, and this cultural pluralism manifested itself in practically every facet of society.

89 The great emperor
Alexius Comnenus,
who exploited
the Crusaders for
his own purposes,
and held off the
Normans, Patzinaks
and Turks
by war or diplomacy

The appearance of the Normans in Italy and the attempt of Guiscard to control both sides of the entrance to the Adriatic Sea greatly alarmed Venice which found its growing maritime power threatened. In consequence the Venetians were glad to accept Alexius' proposal for an alliance against the Normans, particularly as the desperate need of the empire for naval assistance led Alexius to grant the Venetian merchants those formidable commercial privileges in the empire which lay at the basis of the rise of Venice's commercial empire. Nevertheless, the Byzantine maritime city Dyrrachium, the starting point of the Via Aegnatia, fell to Guiscard in 1081 in spite of Venetian aid, and the advance of the Normans seemed irresistible. But a sedition, stimulated by Byzantium, forced Guiscard to return to Italy in 1082, and this diversion enabled the imperial forces to retake Thessaly, while Dyrrachium fell to the Venetians. The death of Guiscard (1085) provided Alexius with a badly-needed respite, for by 1090–91, the Patzinaks, allied with the Turkish emir of Smyrna, were attacking Constantinople by land and sea. The crisis

90 The twelfth-century Norman cathedral at
Cefalù contains this mosaic of Christ, made
by Byzantine craftsmen

91, 92 Byzantine cultural influences were
particularly strong in Venice. These scenes
from the New Testament in ivory (right) and
the mosaic of the Last Supper in St Mark's
(below) show Byzantine aspects of twelfth-
century Venetian art

was acute, but fortunately Alexius, having secured the alliance of the Cumans, inflicted a crushing defeat on the Patzinaks at Mt Levounion in an action which resulted in the almost complete extermination of these nomads. The emperor had weathered the worst of the storm. Alexius could now pause to marshal his strength for the reconquest of Anatolia where the various Turkish chieftains were quarrelling with one another.

The emperor's plans were suddenly jolted when the advance elements of the First Crusade made their way through the Byzantine provinces to Constantinople. At an earlier date Alexius had appealed to the west for aid, but he had envisaged restricted numbers of mercenaries rather than the formidable crusading hosts which had been roused by Pope Urban's preaching at the council of Clermont. In this new confrontation between east and west the differences to which Liudprand had earlier referred soon became painfully evident. Constantinople and Rome, the heirs of the Greeks and the Latins, developed from two different cultures, and historical forces had accentuated their basic differences over the centuries. In the absence of a powerfully organized and centralized state, the papacy had acquired considerably greater freedom of action and political power than had the Greek patriarchate, which was prevented by the existence of a strong secular power in Constantinople from executing the same ambitious policies as its western counterpart.

Friction between the two Churches existed from the fourth century, and as the centuries passed the differences accumulated. The Monophysite problem had resulted in the Acacian schism between pope and patriarch in the fifth century. Later, at the time of the Iconoclastic controversy, Leo III not only alienated the papacy by his proscription of images, but also proceeded to transfer Illyricum and southern Italy from papal to patriarchal jurisdiction. This combined with the Lombard pressures to turn the popes from the Byzantines to the Carolingians – a fateful step. The conversion of the south Slavs, begun under the patriarch Photius, once more led to a temporary break in relations between Rome and Constantinople. By 1024, however, there seems to have been an agreement between the heads of the two Churches that each should be supreme in its own sphere, but the Cluniac movement had the effect of rejuvenating the papacy, providing it with a new *élan*. From the time of Pope Leo IX this new reformatory trend spread rapidly, and wherever its representatives went they enforced a stricter subservience of spiritual life to the papacy. As papal influence spread into the Byzantine regions of southern Italy it encountered resistance from the Greek Church. Finally, the presence of ambitious clerics on the thrones of Rome and Constantinople furnished the spark which ignited the explosive differences separating the Catholic and Orthodox Churches. Pope Leo IX sent the haughty Cardinal Humbert as head of a legation to present the papal point of view to the patriarch Cerularius, who was himself one of the most powerful men ever to hold the patriarchal office. Cerularius displayed an equally imperious temper in handling both emperors and popes and the controversy between the two Churches quickly came to a head. It focused upon minutiae of dogma and ritual – celibacy of the clergy, the use of unleavened bread in communion, fasting on the Sabbath, and the famous clause *filioque* – all concrete points which the popular mind could readily grasp. The intransigence of both sides culminated in 1054, when Humbert arrogantly placed an excommunication of Cerularius on the altar of Hagia Sophia, and Cerularius in turn excommunicated Humbert and his retinue. Though there were no immediate consequences, the schism of the two Churches formalized the differences of east and west, and the political complications of the twelfth century arising from the Crusades soon gave real substance to this religious schism. It is only in the present generation that the Orthodox and Catholic Churches have agreed to withdraw the maledictions they hurled at one another over nine hundred years ago.

The Crusading mentality was coloured by the effect of these religious and cultural differences. Even in the First Crusade, which of all the Crusades was the one most nearly 'pure' in motivation, worldly considerations were present. The Italian cities observed the movement through the eyes of the greedy merchant, while the Normans intended to exploit the Crusade to acquire new lands and victories at the expense of Byzantium. Alexius, faced with the presence of powerful western armies, decided to use them to reconquer

93 The battle of Dorylaum, where Byzantines and Crusaders defeated the Seljuks. This victory enabled them to invade Cilicia (1104)

what he could of Anatolia. In 1096–97 the Crusading leaders gathered in Constantinople where the emperor finally persuaded them to swear an oath, agreeing that all lands formerly belonging to the empire which they might conquer would be returned to Alexius.

In return the emperor would support the westerners in their march.

The bargain which the emperor had struck bore fruit when the defeated Turks surrendered Nicaea to the Byzantines. Shortly thereafter Byzantine forces drove the Turks from the entire western region of Anatolia, but the apparent harmony of Greeks and Crusaders was smashed when Bohemund claimed the city of Antioch for himself in 1098. The Byzantine reconquest of Cilicia (1104) brought Graeco-Norman antagonism to a head once more, and Bohemund, playing upon religious differences, spread propaganda stories that the Greeks had betrayed the Crusade and prepared to invade the empire from the west. This time, however, Alexius was in an entirely different situation from that in which Guiscard had found him in 1081. Bohemund was defeated in western Greece and forced to surrender, ignominiously agreeing to hold Antioch as a fief bestowed by the emperor. Though Alexius had successfully thwarted Norman efforts to destroy the empire, the Norman heritage was to remain a bitter one for the Byzantines throughout the twelfth century, culminating in the Norman sack of Corinth, Thebes, and Thessalonica.

After thirty-seven arduous years as ruler Alexius had greatly strengthened the empire and restored its glory, having found Byzantium virtually destroyed, deprived of its fairest provinces, and with the foes at the door. Through sheer ability he defeated the Normans, destroyed the Patzinaks, exploited the Crusaders, and forced the Turks to retreat. The position of the empire at his death, however, was not that which it had been a century earlier, for unfortunately the reconquest of Anatolia had been incomplete, leaving the central plateau in the hands of the Seljuks, and the defeat of Guiscard had been made possible by the commercial immunities that Alexius gave the Venetians in order to secure their assistance. The inheritance of John II and Manuel I Comnenus was thus an ambivalent one, compounded of empty glory and unpleasant reality. Though it is true that Venice had developed an efficient maritime enterprise by the eleventh century, it was the concessions which it

94 Virgin and Child between the emperor John II Comnenus and the empress Eirene; mosaic of about 1118 in Hagia Sophia

acquired in 1082 that established the basis for its commercial empire and marked the start of Italian encroachment on the empire's economic life. The emperors made repeated but unsuccessful efforts to throw off this stranglehold, but in the end the western merchants were like parasites devouring the empire's strength.

Alexius had granted Venetians the right of trading in the ports of the empire duty free, a concession which put them far beyond competition from Byzantine merchants, who were still required to pay the formidable array of commercial taxes. The unfortunate result was not only that the carrying trade passed from the hands of the Greeks into the hands of the Venetians, but a rich source of revenue was forever alienated from the empire's treasury. Alexius further allotted the Venetians a quarter in Constantinople and three quays with warehouses on the Golden Horn for their ships and merchandise. To the large numbers of western mercenaries who had previously come to Byzantium there was thus added a new influx of Latin merchants whose numbers in twelfth-century Constantinople would eventually attain tens of thousands. The fierce competition

95 Manuel Comnenus, during whose reign Anatolia was effectively lost to Islam

96 Tekfur Saray, a palace in Constantinople, probably built by Manuel Comnenus

of Venice's rivals, coupled with Byzantine fear of an exclusive Venetian commercial monopoly within the empire, led to the granting of similar privileges to Pisa and Genoa as the emperors attempted to play one Italian city off against another.

John II Comnenus attempted to strike a balance between Turkish affairs in Anatolia and the affairs of the west, and he not only consolidated the Anatolian gains of his father but extended them at the expense of the Seljuks. The accession of the more flamboyant Manuel, however, upset this balance, largely because he was hypnotized by the west. He surrounded himself with Latins, adopted Latin customs (he loved to participate in western jousting tournaments), and took as his second wife a Latin princess. He became so deeply engrossed in Italian and German politics that he neglected the defence of the Byzantine Anatolian provinces, allowing Kilij Arslan to eliminate his Danishmend rivals and to make the Seljuk power once more a serious threat. Finally realizing the drastic changes that had taken place in Anatolia, Manuel set out with his armies to attack the Seljuk capital of Konya (ancient Iconium) in 1176.

As the Byzantine armies moved from western Anatolia into the mountain passes leading to the plateau they suffered continuous harassment from the numerous Turkmen tribes that lived on the borders between Seljuks and Greeks. Having arrived in the Phrygian pass of Myriokephalon, Manuel's army suddenly found itself surrounded and the battle that followed was another Manzikert for the Byzantine soldiery, which suffered disaster in this critical encounter. The fighting was obscured by a raging sandstorm during which the slaughter of friend and foe became indiscriminate but after the defeated emperor accepted Kilij Arslan's terms it became evident that in spite of their victory the Turks had also suffered heavy loss. The retreating Byzantines saw large numbers of dead whose facial skin and genitals had been removed by the Turks so that the Greeks would be unable to recognize the extent of the casualties which the Muslim Turks had suffered. Nevertheless, after this defeat the Byzantines renounced any hope of driving the Turks from Asia Minor and during the remainder of the twelfth century the Turkmen tribes, following the rivers from their sources in the mountains to their outlets in the Aegean, mercilessly devastated the regions which the Comnenoi had so meticulously recolonized.

In the west, Serbs and Bulgars took advantage of the chaos which enveloped Byzantine political life in the last quarter of the twelfth century to establish their independence, and Frederick Barbarossa could count on the support of both the Anatolian and Balkan foes of the empire as he marched through these regions on the way to the Holy Land. The degeneration of the empire's relations with the west carried over into the relations between the Latins and Greeks of Constantinople. Manuel, having previously concluded alliances with Pisa and Genoa, decided to strike at the Venetians within the empire, and on 12 March 1171 all Venetians in the empire were arrested and their ships and goods confiscated.

The affluence of the Venetians in Byzantium had created an intolerable situation and finally led to the breach between the empire and the republic. So oppressive was the economic hegemony of the Latins in Constantinople that the inhabitants of the capital sided with Andronicus when he marched on Constantinople in 1183 to seize power from Alexius II and his Latin mother. The riots which broke out in the streets culminated in a brutal attack upon the lives and property of the Latins in the city. There is no doubt that the events of 1171 and 1183 constitute an important landmark leading to the Latin conquest of the city in 1204. The Venetians had extorted the maximum in official concessions and commercial profit, in order to protect and increase their gains; all that remained was military conquest of Constantinople. It seemed momentarily that the Normans would anticipate the Venetians in this respect for they took the city of Thessalonica by storm in 1185 and subjected the inhabitants to merciless treatment. Though the Norman advance on Constantinople was halted, the fate of Thessalonica constituted both revenge for the massacre of the Latins in 1183 and a foretaste of what would happen to the Greeks in 1204.

FLOWERING OF THE ARTS

The era of the Comnenoi and Angeloi, an era of political decline, was nevertheless one in which the arts, especially literature,

97 This mosaic in St Mark's, Venice, shows the appearance of the original church, which was modelled on the Holy Apostles in Constantinople

flourished. Though artistic activity, because of less favourable political and economic factors, was not as extensive as under the Macedonians, Byzantine influence is to be seen in the art of Kievan Russia, Venice, Norman Sicily and the Holy Land. It is perhaps not the least remarkable phenomenon of the late empire that its political degeneration was accompanied by increased literary output and by the high quality, if not quantity, of artistic production. This is in itself an interesting commentary upon the supposed interrelationship between political success and cultural flowering which historians often presuppose.

In contrast to its political fortunes, the literary life of the empire under the Comnenoi and Angeloi represents both continuity with and intensification of the literary life which had developed in the

98 Byzantine art exercised a profound influence over the art of Kievan Russia, particularly through this icon, the Virgin of Vladimir, painted in Constantinople about 1125 and subsequently taken to Russia

eleventh century. Even more than their Macedonian predecessors the scholars and writers of the twelfth century studied and imitated the classical authors, though the traditional religious literature also remained a constant element in the Byzantine cultural picture. It is true that the Church condemned John Italus for daring to equate philosophy with theology, but on the other hand the two greatest classical scholars of the time were archbishops. The erudition of Eustathius of Thessalonica, evident in his voluminous commentaries on the Homeric and Pindaric texts, constitutes a monument in the history of Greek scholarship and the aesthetic receptivity of these cleric-scholars to Greek poetry is clearly stated in the very first line of Eustathius' Homeric commentary. 'If anyone wishes to escape the power of Homer's Sirenes perhaps it would be a good thing for him to smear his ears with wax in order to avoid bewitchment.'

Eustathius' house in Constantinople had become a school in which he educated young men in the classics, his most cultivated student being the future archbishop of Athens, Michael Acominatus. This infatuation with the rich literary testament of the Greeks was an integral element in the Byzantine feeling of cultural superiority over the rest of the world. Anna Comnena repeatedly apologizes for defiling her history with names and words of barbarian origin, whereas Michael Acominatus is a medieval forerunner of those modern classicists who make their pilgrimages to the Acropolis and simultaneously berate contemporary Athenians for lacking the physical and intellectual qualities of Apollo and Plato. An Anatolian disciple of cultural Hellenism born in Phrygia, Michael journeyed to Athens to take up his episcopal duties there and greatly looked forward to his stay among the descendants of Pericles. But it soon became obvious to him, as he preached to the congregation in the Parthenon (now a church dedicated to the Virgin), that the Athens of Pericles was no more. His existence was none the less a pleasant one in contrast to that of another learned archbishop. Theophylact, who had studied at the feet of Psellus, suffered a veritable exile when appointed to the archbishopric of Ochrid in the mountains of the western Balkans. Of what use was literary culture when one was condemned to an audience of croaking frogs and stupid peasants?

The vernacular tongue, as well as classical Greek, found its exponents, and both types of language were employed to relate the sad state of Byzantine society. In spite of the influence of the language and spirit of the great pagan historians, the twelfth-century historians of Byzantium were anything but indifferent to the political and military realities of their time. Far from the spirit of antiquarianism, which preoccupation with classical antiquity so often inspires, Anna Comnena describes in bold strokes the military prowess of the Normans and Latins, filling out her story with detailed observations on Latin superiority in military technology. The historian Choniates stated, without apology, that the chaos of the late twelfth century in parts of Byzantine Anatolia was such that many Greeks preferred to live under the Sultan.

These historians trace the empire's misfortunes clearly and objectively. The poets of Constantinople, though dependent on their tight-fisted patrons, could write social satire as readily as platitudinous encomia, and obviously did so with greater pleasure. Typical was John Tzetzes who recorded some of the flavour of life in Constantinople during the twelfth century. To him Constantinople, perhaps because of its cosmopolitan character, was a city of evil in which thieves and corrupters were canonized as saints. He boasts that on the streets of Constantinople he could greet Scythian, Latin, Persian, Alan, Arab, Russian and Jew each in his own language. The most remarkable of these poets, Theodore Ptochoprodromus, used the vernacular tongue for his stinging comments on social conditions.

The same language had been used by Catacolon Cecaumenus (he notes that he has been criticized for his uneducated Greek) a century earlier in the admonitions which he addressed to his own son and to the emperor. His son is to keep his wife in seclusion lest she, and the family honour, fall victim to the wily arts of the seducer. If he desires long life, he must not keep company with physicians. The poet warns the emperor, among other things, that the employment of barbarian officials will bring evil to the empire. But the vernacular tongue received more artistic treatment at the hands of Ptochoprodromus who used it to complain of perverted social values. In his poem 'Anathema on Letters', for example, he relates how, in

149

spite of long years spent in study, he is in a perpetual state of hunger. Uneducated craftsmen, on the other hand, are well paid, their larders stocked, and their tables graced by fish, stews, roasts, tripe, wine, pure wheat bread and Vlach cheese, while his own pantry is filled exclusively with papers. The artisans' retort was that the poet, who was also a priest, should either satiate his hunger with his verses or else remove his vestments and do some real work, as they did. The complaint of this literary figure that the labourer makes more money is familiarly modern, as is also the anti-clericalism of the workers.

THE FALL OF CONSTANTINOPLE

The ills of Byzantium, apparent in this literature, so weakened the empire that by the end of the twelfth century the end was virtually inevitable. Manuel's schemes had destroyed the strength which Alexius I and John had so laboriously nourished. The Angeloi may have been the nominal successors to the Comnenoi, but they lacked the abilities which the extraordinary position of the empire demanded.

Henry VI, inheritor of a double portion of hatred for the Byzantines (he was a Hohenstaufen who had taken Norman Sicily), had prepared an expedition against the empire which halted only because of his premature death as the fleet was about to sail from Messina in 1197. Two years later at a tournament held on the estates of Count Tibald of Champagne a fiery preacher had inspired the nobles to take the Cross, an event which was very distant from Constantinople and not at all extraordinary in terms of Crusading precedent. The knights obtained support from Pope Innocent III and began to make plans for the invasion of Egypt. With the passing of time, however, direction of the Crusade came progressively under the influence of powerful anti-Byzantine forces.

On the death of Tibald in 1201 leadership of the movement passed into the hands of Boniface of Montferrat, a man with personal interests in both the Holy Land and Byzantium and a strong individual who ended any effective control of the papacy over the Crusade. A friend of the German ruler, Philip of Swabia, he visited the latter's court and undoubtedly had some interesting conversations there. For Philip, married to Irene, the daughter of the dispossessed Byzantine Isaac II, was also host to the young son of Isaac, Alexius. The Crusaders, once arrived in Venice, were unable to raise the 85,000 silver marks which the Venetians had demanded as the price for taking the Crusaders to their destination. But the wily doge, Dandolo, had a very interesting proposition by the acceptance of which the payment of the 85,000 marks could be postponed. The Crusaders should help the Venetians to retake the Dalmatian city of Zara from the Hungarians, and in return Venice would transport the Crusaders to Egypt. The Venetians thus harnessed the Crusaders to their own selfish interests from the beginning. The Crusaders were used to attack a Christian town while only a little earlier the Venetians had entered into negotiations with the ruler of Egypt which were meant to secure Egypt against attack by the Crusaders. After the capture of Zara, Alexius and the Crusaders struck the fatal bargain by which Alexius offered to pay the Crusaders the money owed Venice in return for their aid in restoring his father Isaac to the throne in Constantinople.

The combination of Byzantine dynastic politics, German schemes, and Crusader ambitions had fallen into the hands of Dandolo who now cleverly exploited them to the maximum on behalf of Venetian interests in Byzantium. The Crusaders and Venetians entered Constantinople in the summer of 1203, Isaac was restored to the throne and Alexius crowned co-emperor. But Alexius was not able to fulfil the promises he had made the Crusaders for he lacked money and the people resisted ecclesiastical union with the Latins. The relation of Latins and Greeks now became greatly strained. The former pillaged the Greek villages in the city's environs and burned a portion of the city itself, and the Crusaders and Venetians, having decided to abandon the struggle against the Muslims, made an arrangement for the expected partition of the Byzantine empire. The future emperor, whom they would elect from their own group, would receive the two palaces of Constantinople and one-fourth of the city and empire, the remaining three-quarters to be evenly divided between Venetians and Crusaders. In April 1204, after

Alexius V had removed Isaac and Alexius IV, the Latins attacked the city and this time their victory was complete. The emperor, patriarch, and Theodore Lascaris, along with other Greeks, fled to Asia Minor and the Balkans to organize resistance there, and the Latin soldiery subjected the greatest city in Europe to an indescribable sack. For three days they murdered, raped, looted and destroyed on a scale which even the ancient Vandals and Goths would have found unbelievable. Constantinople had become a veritable museum of ancient and Byzantine art, an emporium of such incredible wealth that the Latins were astounded at the riches they found. Though the Venetians had an appreciation for the art which they discovered (they were themselves semi-Byzantines) and saved much of it, the French and others destroyed indiscriminately, halting to refresh themselves with wine, violation of nuns, and murder of Orthodox clerics. The Crusaders vented their hatred for the Greeks most spectacularly in the desecration of the greatest church in Christendom. They smashed the silver iconostasis, the icons and the holy books of Hagia Sophia, and seated upon the patriarchal throne a whore who sang coarse songs as they drank wine from the church's holy vessels.

The estrangement of east and west, which had proceeded over the centuries, culminated in the horrible massacre that accompanied the conquest of Constantinople. The Greeks were convinced that even the Turks, had they taken the city, would not have been as cruel as the Latin Christians. The defeat of Byzantium, already in a state of decline, accelerated political degeneration so that the Byzantines eventually became an easy prey to the Turks. The Crusading movement thus resulted, ultimately, in the victory of Islam, a result which was of course the exact opposite of its original intention.

IV PROSTRATION AND COLLAPSE

The consequences of the Crusaders' act in the final Islamic victory over the Greek empire were great, but the immediate effects were also significant. Loss of *The City* (ἡ πόλις), as Greeks called Constantinople then and as they call it even today, splintered the unity of medieval Greek society. The Greeks could no longer consider Constantinople, over whose political and religious life a western emperor and a Catholic patriarch presided, as the focal point of their loyalty, though desire for and belief in the ultimate repossession of the city constituted a dominating motive in the Orthodox world. Constantinople was lost, but the empire survived. While the Latins occupied the queen of cities and many of the provinces, Greek nobles, clergy, and soldiers fled in large numbers to those districts which were still free from the Westerners. In these areas, to which mountains or seas barred the Latins from ready access, Greek political entities crystallized around the cities of Nicaea, Trebizond and Arta (in Epirus). The newly-formed kingdoms competed with one another for the allegiance of the Greeks, and their competition to reconquer Constantinople from the Latins somewhat eased the pressure on the latter. The founders of the dynasties which took root in Epirus, Bithynia and Chaldia were all related to imperial families and their dynastic connections greatly enhanced their claims to the obedience of the provincial Greeks. The political splintering of the Byzantine world which resulted from the Latin conquest not only retarded the Greek reconquest of Constantinople but, as it survived long after 1261, further contributed to the final collapse. However, the existence of independent states in Pontus, western Asia Minor and western Greece served to revitalize the Hellenism of those areas, for the rulers did much to foster the economic, religious and cultural life of their subjects.

99 Hagia Sophia in Trebizond

Michael Angelus Comnenus Ducas, founder of the despotate of Epirus, had decided to make his political fortune by joining the Latin conquerors of Greece. But it soon became evident to the Byzantine adventurer that there was very little hope of fulfilling his ambitions as a soldier in the Latin armies, so he turned elsewhere. Relying upon family connections in central and western Greece, Michael Angelus succeeded in taking Arta where he forced the deposed but itinerant Alexius III to crown him despot, thereby dignifying his opportunism with legitimacy. A wily politician and vigorous campaigner who knew how to manipulate Latins and Bulgars, he soon expanded the boundaries of the despotate westward to Dyrrachium and eastward to Thessaly.

Trebizond enjoyed even greater protection from Latin aggrandizement than did Epirus, for it was several hundred miles distant from the Latins, and the city could boast of many other advantages.

Its strategic geographical location made of it one of the great commercial emporia of the east, where Latin and Greek boats met Muslim caravans, bringing profitable income to the Trebizondines. Though the immediate hinterland of the city was not extensive (the Turks ruled the plateau to the south of the mountains) it was well watered and fertile. The Turkish conquest of the plateau had largely isolated Trebizond in the late eleventh century and stimulated separatist sentiment among many of its inhabitants. The most powerful family in the region, that of Gabras, had caused the Comnenoi many anxious moments as they demonstrated their independence quite openly; indeed, the history of this aristocratic clan in the twelfth century is particularly interesting. One Gabras, principal defender of Trebizond against the Turks, was put to death by them for refusing to apostatize, and a special service was sung in his honour as late as the nineteenth century. Paradoxically, another branch of the family furnished three viziers to the Seljuk court at Konya.

100 Wall painting from Hagia Sophia in Trebizond, showing the expulsion of the devil from the daughter of the woman of Canaan

101 The walls of Nicaea

The individuality of the city is further reflected in the pride of its panegyrists who always pointed to its colonization in antiquity by Athenians (via Sinope and Miletus). As in the case of the founder of the Epirote despotate, Alexius and David Comnenus were not only related to an emperor, but their family had strong local connections. Their grandfather, Andronicus I, had governed Sinope, and their aunt was Queen Thamar of Georgia. The two princes had escaped the massacre of Andronicus' family, which accompanied his fall in 1185, and had been raised at the Georgian court. Thamar took advantage of the Latin pressure on Constantinople in 1204 to occupy the city of Trebizond with Georgian troops and then to place her nephews in control of it. David, the more daring of the brothers, soon expanded control over the Pontus Littoral from Trebizond to Heracleia in the west.

It was the third of these Greek succession states, the empire of Nicaea, which was fated to restore Byzantine honour in Constantinople. Unlike Trebizond (which was too far away) and Epirus (which was economically poor), Nicaea enjoyed both a propitious geographical location and the possession of an extensive, fertile hinterland. The rich valleys of western Anatolia, watered by the

102 Ninth-century mosaic (now destroyed) in the Church of the Assumption in Nicaea

103 The emperor Theodore Lascaris, who began the Greek reconquest of the splintered Byzantine empire

104 The coronation of Baldwin of Flanders, emperor of the Latin ▶ states with Venetian support

rivers that streamed down from the mountains, supported a prosperous agricultural life and a dense population, while the important cities of Smyrna, Ephesus, Magnesia, Pergamum, Prusa, Nicomedia and Nicaea gave this region a strong commercial and urban character. The city of Nicaea, closer to Constantinople than Trebizond or Arta, was nevertheless virtually impregnable, located as it was on the shores of Lake Ascania and surrounded by strong walls. In addition it enjoyed the prestige of having been the scene of the first and last of the ecumenical councils recognized by the Greek Church.

The despot Theodore Lascaris was one of those Byzantine officials who had left the capital, preferring to fight on in western Anatolia. The situation in these regions was extremely confused as other Greeks began to establish rival principalities and, more important, Latins, Seljuks and Trebizondines began to press in on all sides. But Theodore obtained a respite to organize his forces after the Latin empire suffered a disastrous defeat at the hands of the Bulgarian monarch Ioannitsa in 1205. Three years later, the Church having elected a new patriarch, Theodore was crowned emperor and so the

imperial traditions took root in the Byzantine polity of Nicaea. Kaihusrau, Sultan of Konya and host of Alexius III, decided to invade the Nicaean domains in 1211, on the pretext of restoring Alexius but actually to conquer the land. In a hotly contested battle which took place near the Maeander River, Theodore killed the Sultan and the victory which followed assured the eastern boundaries of the state. By 1214 peace had been concluded with the Latins and Theodore had reconquered from the Comnenoi the Black Sea coast as far east as Sinope.

THE LATIN ADMINISTRATION

The Latin settlement of those lands which had been successfully wrested from the Greeks was a complex one. The Doge Dandolo, who had feared the ambitions of Boniface, saw to it that a weaker man, Baldwin of Flanders, was elected emperor, while the Venetian Thomas Morosini was chosen patriarch. The partition of the conquest proceeded according to the general lines previously agreed upon. Baldwin received Thrace, five-eighths of Constantinople, northwest Asia Minor, and a few of the islands. His frustrated competitor Boniface took the important city of Thessalonica with adjacent lands in Macedonia and Thessaly, giving Attica and Boeotia to his vassal, Otto de la Roche. The Venetians, political realists that they were, claimed only those regions which would constitute no liability for their commercial interests, the most important being the section of Constantinople (three-eighths) which they received. In addition they acquired Dyrrachium, Ragusa (on the Dalmatian coast), Coron, Modon (in the southern Peloponnese), certain ports on the Hellespont and Marmora, and the city of Adrianople. In terms of actual territory the Ionian islands, Crete, and the isles of the Aegean constituted the bulk of their holdings.

The Peloponnese, or Morea as it was called, capitulated to William of Champlitte and Geoffrey of Villhardouin. Spectacular as the victory of the Latins had been, the congeries of Latin states which arose represented a dismally weak political system which could exist only because of the threefold division of the Greeks. The Crusaders superimposed a developed western feudal system over their new lands which produced a fatal decentralization of power. Though all the knights held their lands from the emperor of Constantinople, the interests of the Latins in the provinces often diverged from his. And the Venetians had been careful to stipulate that they were not required to swear the oath of fealty to the emperor, a factor which further weakened the Latin empire.

The basic weakness of the new Latin states lay in the fact that the subject population was largely Greek and so loyalty to the ruling class was largely, though not universally, absent. Ecclesiastical differences cemented the hatred of the Greeks for their new masters, for one of the basic policies of the Latins was to establish the ecclesiastical supremacy of the Catholic Church. Pope Innocent III, excited by the prospect of bringing the Greek Church into the Catholic fold, was outraged by the massacre and rapine which accompanied the Latin entry into Constantinople, and repeatedly admonished Latin clerics and lords to treat the Greeks in a more Christian manner, but usually to no avail.

A number of the Greek bishops, including the patriarch of Constantinople and the famous archbishop of Athens, Michael

Acominatus, had fled the Latin-held lands, seeking refuge in Epirus, Nicaea, Bulgaria and Trebizond. Others remained in their sees, sometimes ignoring Latin ecclesiastical demands and often maintaining contact with the clergy in non-Latin territory. The Catholics decided that the Greek clergy were to keep the churches in those regions inhabited exclusively by Greeks, but in mixed areas the bishops were to be Latins. The hierarchy of the Church in the conquered areas thus passed into the hands of the Catholics, whereas the village priests remained Greek. With some exceptions the Latin bishoprics were filled by adventurers little inspired by the religious life, who treated their Greek parishioners as schismatics. Very often the Greek clergy who conformed to the demands of the papacy and hence were supported by Innocent, were removed by fanatic Latin bishops who wished to take over all the bishoprics.

The Greek bishops were often equally irreconcilable. The archbishop of Corfu, for example, roundly told the Crusaders who stopped there *en route* for Constantinople in 1203 that he could not understand their arguments in favour of papal primacy unless they were referring to the fact that it was Roman soldiers who had crucified Christ. Nevertheless, in spite of their great political animosity, the Nicaean Greeks and the Latins did engage in religious discussions, the most important of which were held in Constantinople (1206, 1214–15). The appearance of Nicholas Mesarites, metropolitan of Ephesus, as the Greek representative undoubtedly helped to strengthen the resistance of the Greeks in Constantinople, but it did little to improve relations between the two Churches. The hostility and rigidity of Catholic and Orthodox extended even to details of protocol and procedure. The dispute between the papal cardinal and Mesarites over precedence is a case in point. When Mesarites entered Hagia Sophia the cardinal failed to rise in greeting, alleging that as he wore purple slippers, to rise would be unbecoming to the imperial dignity which attached to the wearing of purple. The metropolitan of Ephesus was not to be outdone, however, and pulling off his slipper, displayed that its lining was purple also. Being more humble than his Latin adversary, he claimed, he had naturally refrained from a more ostentatious display of the purple!

The intercourse of Greeks and Latins was perhaps less agitated in spheres other than the religious. The fusion of Byzantine and Frankish elements in the Peloponnese is reflected in the so-called Chronicle of the Morea, the text of which exists in Greek, French, Aragonese, and Italian. The Greek magnates of the peninsula joined with the Latin knights and formed one feudal society. The Byzantine *pronoia* was equated with the Frankish fief, and the two terms were used interchangeably in the Chronicle. Latin feudalism was thus grafted on to the Byzantine land-holding system and such Latin terms as *liege* (already known in the relations between Comnenoi and the Crusading lords) and *homage* passed into Greek by transliteration (*lizios*) and translation (*anthropea*).

The same sort of accommodation seems to have occurred in the field of literature. Greek and French romance literature followed a similar evolution, and just as parallel developments in Byzantine and Latin feudalism had prepared the way for a fusion of the two, so a fusion took place in the case of this type of literature. There was also a direct influence of the French romance on that of the Byzantines as the latter developed in the thirteenth and subsequent centuries.

The preponderance of the west in economic life, so evident in the twelfth century, was now firmly established. The influence of the Italian merchants became so great that the maritime and mercantile vocabularies, not only of Greek, but later of Turkish as well, were largely Italian. The results of this Latin dominance were strongest in those Venetian insular possessions which remained under western rule until the late eighteenth century. Though proselytization by the Catholic Church failed to attain the same degree of success in the Ionian islands as in certain of the islands of the Aegean, the cultural borrowing of the Ionian islanders was very extensive. The most felicitous blending of the two strains is to be seen in the great school of Cretan painting, which continued in the Ionian islands after the Turkish conquest of Crete in the seventeenth century caused the painters to disperse. The literature of the islanders also experienced a new flowering under the inspiration of Italian models. The Italian

105 St Luke and St James, painted in Constantinople, probably in the thirteenth century; from an Acts and Epistles ▶

106 The great bronze horses of St Mark's, brought to Venice after the sack of Constantinople

imprint on the Ionian islands was so strong that their inhabitants had a different outlook from that of their compatriots on the mainland even as late as the nineteenth century.

The most obvious type of Latin 'borrowing' from the Greeks consisted of the objects of classical and Byzantine art which came into Europe after 1204, the most famous of which are the great bronze horses standing over the entrance to St Mark's in Venice. Constantinople, the great repository of holy relics, now became the supply house for all Europe. More exceptional was the case of William of Moerbeke, archbishop of Corinth (1277–81), who translated many of Aristotle's works into Latin. But as interest in the reunion of the two Churches spread in the west, the desire to learn Greek was motivated more by religious than by other considerations.

RECONQUEST OF CONSTANTINOPLE

In the competition between the Balkan and Asiatic Greeks to reconquer Constantinople fortune at first favoured the despotate of Epirus. Theodore Angelus, successor of Michael Angelus, took

Thessalonica from the Latins in 1224 and had himself crowned emperor soon afterwards by the archbishop of Ochrid. His defeat at the hands of the Bulgarian Tsar Asen II on the field of Klokotinitza in 1230 put an abrupt end to Epirote imperial pretensions. Until his death in 1241 Asen enjoyed a certain pre-eminence in Balkan affairs, but it was the Nicaeans who finally began to extend their control in Thrace and Macedonia.

Under the leadership of John III Ducas Vatatzes (1222–54) the empire of Nicaea emerged as the most powerful of the Greek states, playing a rôle which was something more than local. Vatatzes concluded a marriage alliance with Frederick II, talked with the pope of union, and concluded an agreement with the Seljuks in the face of the Mongol storm. Internally he succeeded in restoring great prosperity to his Anatolian realm. A tariff policy which protected local manufactures against Italian competition revived the old Byzantine textile industry, while the warehouses of the ports were full of goods from all over the world. He paid particular attention to the towns, filling their silos with agricultural products and maintaining at state expense craftsmen who specialized in the making of arms. Education also profited as he brought together collections of books in the various cities. His reign demonstrates the advantageous side of that splintering which the Latin conquest of 1204 had caused, for prior to that date the Byzantine capital had neglected its fairest province. Furthermore, his extension of Nicaean power in the Balkans, crowned by the occupation of Thessalonica in 1246, isolated the Latins in Constantinople, and made the final reconquest only a matter of time.

The final triumph was, ironically, not to be the work of the Lascarid dynasty, for in 1258 Michael Palaeologus, descendent of an old aristocratic family, seized effective control of power and founded the most long-lived of the Byzantine imperial dynasties. At this juncture the rapid progress of the Anatolian Greeks had inspired their enemies to come together in a last effort to thwart their further advance. Manfred, the son of Frederick II, put himself at the head of a coalition which also included the despotate of Epirus and the Latin principality of the Morea. The fateful battle at Pelagonia in western Greece (1259) was a smashing victory for Michael Palaeologus, which left him free not only to concentrate on Constantinople, but also to advance in the Morea. In order to neutralize the Venetian navy, the only force still capable of effective resistance, Michael secured Genoese support by the treaty of Nymphaeum, which guaranteed Genoese merchants very handsome commercial rewards within the empire. But Genoese aid proved unnecessary, for a small body of Nicaean troops, reconnoitring in the neighbourhood of Constantinople, found the city undefended and took it with ease on 25 June 1261. In the joyous celebration which followed, Michael had himself crowned anew by the patriarch, this time in Hagia Sophia. In this way the traditions of Constantinople as head of the Greek empire and Church were renewed.

The expulsion of the hated Franks from Constantinople was a great victory for Byzantium, but in other ways it was a source of ill fortune. Once in possession of Constantinople, Michael found himself involved not only with the various Balkan states, but above all with Latin Crusaders who hoped to re-establish the Latin empire of Constantinople. Furthermore, in shifting the capital to Europe, Michael turned his back on western Anatolia and neglected the very provinces which had made the reconquest possible. The neglect of these regions at the very moment when Turkish pressure was once more increasing was to prove fatal. The more immediate danger, however, came from developments in the west where the ambitious Charles of Anjou, brother of the French King Louis IX, had won the kingdom of Sicily from Manfred. By the treaty of Viterbo (1267) with Baldwin II, the deposed emperor of Constantinople, Charles began to muster allies for an expedition against Constantinople. His diplomacy built up connections with the Latin Morea, Epirus, the Bulgars and the Serbs, and for fifteen years Michael VIII lived under the threat of a Latin Crusade. Fortunately Byzantine diplomatic skill prevented Charles from launching his Crusade. As a first step Michael concluded an ecclesiastical union with the Latin Church at Lyons in 1274, accepting papal supremacy in return for which the pope compelled Charles to desist from his plans. The succession of the French pope Martin IV gave Charles another opportunity, and he was on the point of unleashing his forces when the outbreak of the Sicilian Vespers (1282) put an end to his schemes. Byzantine gold was used to encourage discontent in Sicily and brought the forces of Peter III of Aragon into the island.

Michael VIII had succeeded in raising Byzantium once more to a position of world prominence by virtue of his spectacular victories over the Latins. But the accomplishment was ephemeral, and the possession of Constantinople proved to be a burden beyond the means of a government which had abandoned its real base of strength in Asia Minor in order to pursue a deceptive policy of glory in the Balkans. Though the consequences of Michael's policy were not fully revealed during his lifetime, the fact remained that, having plunged into the political world of the Balkans and the west, the Byzantine state could not turn back, although it was physically unequal to the task. Furthermore, Michael's dynastic, military and economic policies reduced Byzantine Anatolia to a rebellious province in which the native soldiery was disbanded, agricultural life dislocated, and the ecclesiastical hierarchy alienated.

107 Tower at Galata, the citadel of the Genoese merchant community, established in Constantinople as part-payment for Genoese help against the Latin states

108, 109 Michael VIII Palaeologus (left), who rekindled the last embers of Byzantine power; and his unlucky successor, Andronicus II (right)

Andronicus II (1282–1328) harvested the bitter fruit of Michael's labours, for though he succeeded to the throne in Constantinople rather than in Nicaea he found the state exhausted by Michael's policies. The story of the empire after the death of Michael VIII becomes a tale of military disaster, economic decline, and political catastrophe which makes melancholy reading. The pretensions of Michael had subjected the empire to increasing demands at a time when its resources were diminishing. When he usurped the imperial power Michael had sought to satisfy his military and aristocratic supporters by making their *pronoia* or fiefs hereditary. This set a precedent, and during the next two centuries there was a steady increase in the number of hereditary *pronoia*, often accompanied by freedom from military service. At the same time the Palaeologoi granted an increasing number of tax exemptions to the possessors of non-military lands, with the result that tax revenues and military

110 The emperor John VI Cantacuzene enthroned, with bishops and monks, at a council summoned by him in 1351

personnel steadily decreased. Customs revenue also shrank, as a consequence of the stranglehold of the Genoese and Venetians over the economic life of the empire. While by the fourteenth century the annual customs revenues of the Genoese in Galata reached the sum of 200,000 hyperpera, across the Golden Horn in Constantinople the Greeks levied only 30,000 hyperpera. It is estimated that at the end of the thirteenth century the income of the state was only one-eighth of what it had been under the Isaurian dynasty. This impoverishment even affected the sumptuous court ceremonial; at the coronation of John VI Cantacuzene, for example, the gold and silver plate was replaced by plate of lead and clay.

Dynastic competition, social struggles and religious strife during the fourteenth century destroyed what little strength the empire possessed and played into the hands of the Serbs and Ottoman Turks. In 1321 Andronicus III, grandson of Andronicus II, raised the spectre of dynastic rebellion by marching on the capital and forcing his grandfather to give him part of Macedonia and Thrace. When the family strife was renewed the two emperors sought support from the Serbs and the Bulgars. The sins of Andronicus III were visited upon his own younger son John V, for upon the latter's accession John Cantacuzene had himself declared emperor. During the next fourteen years the empire suffered the horrors of intense civil war, and once again the rival parties, placing their own political interests above the welfare of the state, competed for the services of Serbs, Turks, and Venetians.

The religious controversy over Hesychasm further paralysed society in the mid-fourteenth century as the exponents of Hesychast doctrine sided with Cantacuzene and the opponents with John V. The controversy arose when the westerner Barlaam attacked the mystical exercises of the monks of Mount Athos and Gregory Palamas came to their defence. The hesychast attained mystical ecstasy by sitting on his legs, head on chest and eyes focused on the navel, invoking the name of Jesus as he held his breath. By this exercise the mystic saw the uncreated light which surrounded Jesus at the Transfiguration on Mount Tabor. The conflict was not only theological, it also represented another phase in the continuing encounter between Byzantine monasticism and humanistic tradi-tions. Hesychasm was vindicated because of the support it received from Cantacuzene, but eventually it was restricted to a small number of ascetics.

Nevertheless, this last great theological debate of the Eastern Church was important in so far as it contributed to the anarchy and confusion of Byzantine society which the civil wars had caused. In the course of the struggle the regency of John V also fomented class strife at the expense of Cantacuzene, who represented the aristocracy of Byzantine society. Because of the civil war and political and economic decline, the gap separating the rich from the poor had greatly widened and at the prodding of the government of John V the lower classes (the political zealots) rose in the towns of Thrace and Macedonia, establishing their own municipal government in Thessalonica and expelling the aristocrats.

When John Cantacuzene finally fell from power in 1354 and retired to a monastery to write his famous history, he left the empire in a shambles. Society had been split along dynastic, social and religious lines, while Serbs and Turks had not only been allowed to expand at the expense of Byzantium but had been brought in as mercenaries. The years of civil war had seriously dislocated Byzantine society, disrupting agriculture and destroying the tax-producing elements in the provinces.

Exploiting this weakness the Serbian ruler Milutin (1282–1321) had by the end of the thirteenth century pushed ahead with the conquest of Macedonia south of Skoplje. The civil wars of the fourteenth century brought the Serbs as far south as Thessaly and Aetolia after they had eliminated their Bulgarian neighbours at the battle of Velbužd (1330). The Serbian involvement in Byzantine affairs, which began during the civil war of Andronicus II and Andronicus III, reached a high point during the reign of the great Serbian ruler Stephan Dušan (1331–55). Dušan first concluded an alliance with Cantacuzene in 1342–43, but soon abandoned him for John V in order to further his own interests. As Cantacuzene turned towards Constantinople and abandoned Macedonia, Dušan occupied most of Albania, and of central and northern Greece, and in 1346 the Serbian patriarch crowned him emperor of the Serbs and Greeks. Like the Bulgarian ruler Symeon during the tenth century, Dušan attempted to found an empire on the Byzantine pattern, but his effort was short-lived for on his death (1355) the Serbian empire collapsed and was replaced by a number of petty states.

THE RISE OF THE TURKS

The real danger, however, lay not in the Balkans but in Asia Minor. Here were the bellicose Turks who, having inherited the doctrine of holy war from the faltering Arabs, were to carry the centuries-old conflict between Byzantine Christendom and Islam to a conclusion. Turkish conquest and rule, by now three hundred years old in much of Anatolia, had effected great changes in the peninsula. Prior to the battle of Manzikert the population of Asia Minor had consisted largely of Greeks and Armenians, and even as late as the

171

mid-thirteenth century they outnumbered their Turkish neighbours. But with the establishment of the Muslim Turks in the peninsula the Christians of Asia Minor were subject to relentless cultural pressures, for, as the Arab historian Ibn Khaldun observed, 'A nation that has been defeated and comes under the rule of another nation will quickly perish.'

The Turkish conquests and settlements in Anatolia had caused considerable upheaval, dislocation and destruction among the Christians, and the peninsula was not to be pacified until the latter half of the fifteenth century. The Church in particular was crushed as it lost its properties, churches and income, and was subjected to heavy taxation in the period prior to the unification of Anatolia by Muhammed II. The Orthodox Christians, cut off from the heart of their society and deprived of effective Christian leadership (for the bishops were excluded from their sees in Turkish lands for long periods), were exposed to strong proselytizing currents in the new Islamic society. Because of the upheavals which Christian society had experienced, the Dervish orders, most prominent of which were the Mevlevis and Bektashis, found the Christians psychologically

111, 112 Jalal al-din Rumi (left), fourteenth-century sufi and ascetic, was the spiritual founder of the Mevlevi order of Dervishes, who are shown (right) during part of their ritual dance ('sema'). The liberal Mevlevis played an important rôle in the Islamization of the Anatolian Christians

وفرمودهاند که مرغی که از زمین بالا پرد که چه باشد با آسمان نرسد اما اینقدر باشد که از ادم

دورتر باشد و بر همه مجنن اکسی درویش شود و بکمال درویشی نرسد اما اینقدر باشد

که از مروه خلق و اهل باز و رحمتاز زبان باشد و از زحمتهای نیا بر هده و پس یکبار که د که نجی المخففون

و هلاک المثقلون یکی را بنای نیا پیش حضرت مولوی عذ خواسی بیکرد که در خدمت

prepared for their religious preaching. These sufi brotherhoods were thus instrumental in transforming the majority of the Greek and Armenian Christians into Turkish Muslims, and in so doing they effected a cultural revolution equivalent in magnitude to that which the Arabs had carried through centuries earlier in Byzantine Syria, Egypt and Palestine.

The political life of Anatolia had been temporarily stabilized with the establishment of the empire of Nicaea and the emergence of a strong sultanate of Konya in the first half of the thirteenth century. But the withdrawal of Michael VIII to Constantinople in 1261 once more relegated western Anatolia to administrative chaos and economic decline. Meanwhile, on the Islamic side, Seljuk prosperity was destroyed when the rebellions of the Turkmen tribes so weakened the sultanate that it fell a victim to the Mongols in 1243. The disappearance of these two stabilizing forces once more turned Anatolia into a battlefield of Turkish chieftains who, at the head of various combinations of tribes, carved out a number of petty Turkish principalities as they overran the Seljuk and Byzantine domains. The most important of these emirates, that of Osman, was located in northwest Anatolia on the borders of Byzantine Bithynia. By the early fourteenth century, Osman was able to exploit the decline of Byzantine control to conquer most of this region, and his son Orhan rounded out the conquest by reducing Prusa (1326), Nicaea (1331), and Nicomedia (1337).

After a few decades of consolidation, in which the Christian and Muslim elements and institutions of Bithynia fused to produce early Ottoman society, the Ottoman Turks crossed the Dardenelles to Europe much as the Nicaean Greeks had done during the thirteenth century. Cantacuzene had secured the help of Turkish troops in the civil war by giving his daughter in marriage to the Sultan Orhan in 1344–45, and introduced them into Thrace where they plundered the populace mercilessly. Ten years later, after a fearful earthquake had destroyed the walls of Gallipolis, Orhan seized this key town on the European side of the straits and the Turkish conquest of the Balkans began. The collapse of Dušan's empire, together with the weakness of Bulgaria and Byzantium, created a power

,113 A sketch by Gentile Bellini of one of the Janissaries, élite troops recruited by the Ottomans from Christian children who were converted to Islam and maintained as a permanent professional army

vacuum which literally sucked the Turks into Europe. By 1365 they had shifted their capital from Prusa to the European city of Adrianople, symbolizing in this manner the westward orientation of their political programme. Though the Turks bypassed the city of Constantinople because of its defensive strength their advance subdued the Bulgars and then brought the Serbs to their knees at the battle of Kossovo in 1389. The Sultans had succeeded because of the weakness of their opponents but also because they had created the most formidable military machine in all of Europe and the Near East. Much of the vitality of both the military and the administration derived from the system by which the Ottomans took the cream of the Christian youth, converted them to Islam, and then trained them to wield the sword and the pen. The crack troops, the Janissaries, and eventually the viziers were recruited from these converted Christian youths, the *devshirmes*.

When Bayezid I Yildirim, the Thunderbolt, succeeded his father
Murad I and expanded deep into both the Balkans and Anatolia,
the days of the empire grew shorter. Bayezid's conquests in Europe
were put to a severe test by the appearance of a crusading force
under Sigismund of Hungary. Though the initial impact of the
western knights at the battle of Nicopolis (1396) alarmed the Ottoman ranks, the forces of the Sultan annihilated the Crusaders. This
victory proved that the Sultan's position in the Balkans was firmly
established, and Manuel II Palaeologus, fearing that the end was in
sight, left his capital in 1399 and went to Venice, London, and Paris
to seek aid. Only a miracle could now save Constantinople, im-
mersed as it was in an Ottoman sea. Once more in its long history,
however, a miracle did occur and the life of Greek Constantinople

was prolonged another half century. For in 1402 Bayezid met his master at the battle of Angora where the last great world conqueror in the steppe tradition, Timur (Tamerlane), crushed the Ottomans and almost destroyed their empire. But Byzantium was too weak to take advantage of this opportunity and the west was still smarting from the defeat at Nicopolis. Thus, the opportunity passed and capable Ottoman sultans restored the unity and vigour of the young state. The most the empire could do was once again to negotiate ecclesiastical union with Rome (1438–39), but to no practical avail. The union was violently received in the empire and as far away as Kiev the Slav ruler imprisoned the metropolitan of Kiev for having signed the document of union and betrayed the Orthodox cause. The union divided the Byzantine world in the final hour without resulting in any significant material aid from the west.

115, 116 Andrew Palaeologus, despot of the Morea, from a fresco by Pinturicchio (below left); and John VIII Palaeologus portrayed in the famous fresco of Benozzo Gozzoli in the Medici Palace, Florence

THE LITERATURE OF DECLINE

In spite of the civil wars and military disasters which destroyed the empire, both art and literature flourished in the Palaeologan period. Though the obscurantist monastic outlook which was hostile to the classics persisted, the interest of Byzantine intellectuals now turned from the form of classical literature to its content. The Byzantine humanists studied Plato and Homer not only for the richness of their language but also because they found the subject-matter interesting and edifying; in short, they were intellectually sympathetic to the qualities and virtues which the ancient authors described. The university in Constantinople was once more reconstituted, and when Manuel II Palaeologus returned from his journey to the west he reformed it in the light of what he had seen at the Sorbonne.

Thessalonica, already distinguished as a centre of classical studies in the twelfth century, and Mistra were also important for their schools and intellectual activity. Mistra, the Byzantine capital of the Morea, became the focal point of a Greek national and intellectual revival under the political leadership of the Palaeologan princes and sustained by the literary activity of George Gemisthus Pletho. It is

117 Mistra, a hill town in the Peloponnese, much as it was in the fourteenth century

118 The entry into Jerusalem; detail of a wall-painting (c. 1380) in the Church of the Peribleptos, Mistra

interesting that Greek consciousness and cultural life were once more centred in their original homeland after having moved eastward during the Hellenistic-Roman and Byzantine eras. The conquests of Alexander and the rule of the Caesars had made Alexandria and Antioch the centres of Hellenism; later Constantine had made Constantinople the centre of the Greek-speaking world. After the Arab invasions Anatolia had become the heartland of Orthodox society, but the Turks, having reinvigorated the military power of Islam, erased the Greek character of Asia Minor, with the result that Greece once more became the centre of the Greek world.

The most spectacular aspect of Palaeologan intellectual life was the contact and exchanges between the Greek and Italian humanists of the fourteenth and fifteenth centuries. Though relations between Italy and Byzantium had become much closer since the eleventh century, these had been largely political and economic. Thanks to the rise of humanistic scholarship in the west and in the east, however, scholars of both worlds began to be interested in each other's litera-ture. Greek scholars began to translate Latin works into their own language and it is significant that they chose profane as well as

179

religious compositions. The fourteenth-century scholar and ambassador to Venice, Maximus Planudes, translated works by Cato, Ovid, Cicero and Caesar, and Demetrius Cydones rendered into Greek such important theological treatises as the *Summa Theologica* of Thomas Aquinas and the anti-Islamic polemical tract of Ricoldo da Monte Croce. This latter became the principal source for Byzantine knowledge of Islamic doctrine.

But the Italy of Petrarch and Boccaccio thirsted more for Greek literature than did the Greeks for Latin. When the Greek humanist Manuel Chrysolorus accepted an invitation to lecture in Florence on Greek language and literature he was enthusiastically received, and after his return to Constantinople in the early fifteenth century Italian students soon followed him there. The interest of the Italians in learning Greek was motivated not only by pure humanism, for there was also the burning issue of religious union as well as economic and political involvement in the east. Religious and scholarly motivations momentarily fused, however, when the Byzantine emperor, accompanied by Greek scholars and clergy, came to Florence to effect the ecclesiastical union of 1439. The Italian humanists were enthralled by the arrival of such learned classicists as Bessarion and Pletho, and their presence in Italy gave a considerable impetus to the progress of Greek studies.

Greek literati of this late period became increasingly conscious of the empire's decline and reflected this in their writing. One of the most brilliant of the humanists, the bureaucrat Theodore Metochites (d. 1332), had experienced the civil strife of Andronicus II and Andronicus III and had followed closely the Ottoman conquest of Bithynia. He clearly perceived the ever-widening disparity between imperial ceremony and pretensions in Constantinople and the grim reality of the empire's position. The only cure for the melancholy which this perception inspired, he wrote, would be to remain ignorant of the empire's past greatness. But since the historical monuments of past greatness could not be ignored, Metochites sought consolation in ruminating on the rôle of Chance (*Tyche*). The lives of men and nations, he said, are governed by uncertainty and oscillations.

119 Theodore Metochites, humanist writer and bureaucrat, shown holding the Church of Kariye Jami, which was decorated under his patronage

Nations which formerly ruled over others were then enslaved in their turn. This was the case with the Assyrians who became subject to the Persians, just as the Persians and all their subjects become subject to the Macedonians, and the Macedonians to the Romans. And these events occur in an alternating fashion according to chance of time and Tyche. Nor is there anything constant in human affairs nor unchangingly eternal. Just as every individual man or animal suffers birth, growth, decay and destruction and death, thus is it also in human affairs, governments, and dynasties. They also are in constant flux and change, and never constant. They come into being, progress, and then, gradually decaying and changing into the opposite state, they come to an end and die.

It was this reversal of fortune common to all states which, according to Metochites, had overtaken Byzantium.

These sad conditions inspired literary satire in the vernacular tongue, which ridiculed far more crudely than Metochites the unrealistic tone of much of Byzantine traditionalism. By the fifteenth century the empire had become so insignificant that historians such as Chalcocondyles and Critoboulos took as the subject of their narratives not Byzantium but the Ottoman Turks. Other men of letters, not resigned to the approaching end, recommended positive programmes of action. The Latinophile Bessarion proposed what historians today would call 'westernization', for he recommended that Greek youths be sent to the west to study western technology. Pletho conjured up a new Greek state, along Platonic lines, which should be founded in the Peloponnese and which should return to paganism. But despite these 'secular' explanations and proposals Byzantine society retained its religious outlook to the very end and sought an essentially religious explanation for the catastrophic turn of events. Preachers told their congregations that God had sent the Turks to serve as divine chastisement of the sinful Christians. The most famous and sulphuric of these Byzantine preachers was Joseph Bryennius, the violence of whose sermons matched the very violence of the Turkish conquest.

Our rulers are unjust, those who oversee our affairs are rapacious, the judges accept gifts, the mediators are liars, the city dwellers are deceivers, the rustics are unintelligible, and all are useless. Our virgins are more shameless than prostitutes, the widows more curious than they ought to be, the married women disdain and keep not faith, the young men are licentious and the aged drunkards. The nuns have insulted their calling, the priests have forgotten God, the monks have strayed from the straight road. . . . Many of us live in gluttony, drunkenness, fornication, adultery, foulness, licentiousness, hatred, jealousy, envy, and theft. We have become arrogant, braggarts, avaricious, selfish, ungrateful, disobedient, deserters, robbers, traitors, unholy, unjust, unrepentant, irreconcilable. . . . It is these things and other things like them which bring upon us the chastisements of God.

Whatever the causes of decline, be they the instability of human affairs, the virtues of the Turks, or the sins of the Greeks, it is remarkable that even at this late date the outlook of society was not fatalistic. For implicit in the explanation of Byzantine decline was the possibility of reversing the unfortunate state of Christian society. *Tyche* was not constant, sins could be abandoned and the virtuous life resumed, and Greek folklore expressed the common belief that eventually the Turks would be removed.

Though literary activity in a period of stress can be explained by the stimulating effect of political and military crises, these same conditions often exercise a deleterious effect on artistic output and development. For in periods of disaster survival becomes the primary concern of society and the energies, time, and money which art demands are not available. It is therefore extraordinary that Palaeologan art stands out as one of the really great achievements of Byzantine society. The high quality of this art is spectacularly revealed in the Church of the Chora (Kariye Jami) which, under the patronage of Theodore Metochites, was embellished with brilliant mosaics and exquisite frescoes, though it is to be seen also in the monuments of Thessalonica, Mistra, and Serbia.

120, 121 The age of the Palaeologues witnessed a last great flowering of Byzantine art. The mosaics in the Church of Kariye Jami, which include this Christ Pantocrator (above), are particularly notable. The new humanistic approach is seen in this portrait (left) from a manuscript of Hippocrates, c. 1342

122, 123 The naturalistically
depicted shepherds (left)
come from a mosaic (*c.* 1312)
in the Church
of the Holy Apostles
(below left) in Salonica,
an important cultural centre

124 Hagia Maria Pammarkaristos
(below right) is one of the best
surviving later Byzantine exteriors
in Constantinople

125 The Anastasis: Christ descending into Hell and raising Adam and Eve from the dead.
Detail of a wall painting in Kariye Jami, *c.* 1310

The approaching end of the drama could be delayed no longer. Thanks to the rule of the energetic Murad II (1421–51) the Ottoman empire was once more firmly established in both the Balkans and Anatolia, and it only remained for Muhammed II to provide the new empire with its logical capital, Constantinople. In spite of its complete isolation, Constantinople still presented formidable obstacles to Muhammed who realized that the city could not be easily reduced. Therefore he built the fortress of Rumeli Hisar at the narrow point on the Bosphorus so that he might block the grain ships sailing to Constantinople. Muhammed was also concerned as to how he might breach the great land walls which barred his entrance into the city. It was the great misfortune of the Byzantine emperor to lose the services of his Transylvanian cannon-maker Urbanus, who deserted to Muhammed and built some extraordinary pieces both for Rumeli Hisar and for the coming siege of Constantinople.

Constantine XI did what little he could with the meagre resources at hand. He appealed to Pope Nicholas V for aid and the result was the last temporary ecclesiastical union of the two Churches in 1452. The *megadux* Lucas Notaras and the anti-unionists denounced the act and declared that they would prefer to see the Turkish turban rather than the Latin tiara in Constantinople, but many of the people of Constantinople dissented stating that they would rather see the city in the hands of the Latins, who at least professed a belief in Christ. Thus the union divided the Greeks at this critical hour while failing to bring them the necessary aid from the west.

Muhammed deployed his troops before the land walls of Constaninople on Friday, 6 April 1453, and so commenced the last siege of Constantinople by barbarian armies. The struggle was unequal because the Ottoman forces, which conservative estimates place at 80,000, far outnumbered both the total number of the emperor's forces (a mere 9,000) and the population of Constantinople itself (probably less than 50,000). The first bombardment of the city began on 11 April and the naval attack of the Ottoman fleet on 19 April was thwarted by the *megadux* Notaras at the iron chains blocking the entrance to the Golden Horn. The failure of the Ottomans to force the chains and bring their fleet into the Golden Horn was serious, for it meant that the Greeks and Genoese could concentrate their scanty manpower on the land walls where the bulk of the Ottoman army was situated. But on the night of 22 April the Ottomans hauled their ships from the Bosphorus over the hill of Galata and to the accompaniment of rolling drums and screeching trumpets slid them into the waters of the Golden Horn.

Now the sea walls were exposed to Muslim attack and the emperor had to divert soldiers from the land walls to man the extensive walls along the northern shore of Constantinople. Even though this was a great Turkish success, the siege dragged on through the month of May and Muhammed offered Constantine terms by which the emperor could abandon Constantinople for the Morea. Constantine chose the path of honour and informed the Sultan that he preferred

126, 127 Rumeli Hisar (above), fort built on the Bosphorus by Muhammed II (opposite)

to die defending the capital. Muhammed therefore prepared a final assault and on 27 May inspected his troops, personally assigning each body its position. On the morning of the next day the Byzantines worked feverishly to repair breaches in the walls, litanical processions filled the streets, and miraculous icons were placed on the walls. The emperor, surrounded by Greeks and Latins, proceeded to Hagia Sophia where they heard the last Christian mass of the Byzantine empire and then returned to their positions on the walls.

The first Turkish assault, which began on the evening of 28 May, was repulsed but was followed by a second and more determined attack by the Anatolian soldiery. After they had been repelled, Muhammed ordered a third and final attack by the crack Janissaries on the morning of 29 May. During this attack the Genoese general, Giustiniani Longo, was mortally wounded and suddenly the Sultan's standards were seen to float at one point inside the walls. The emperor and his troops continued to resist at the St Romanus gate where Constantine was slain by the Turks.

The Turks had finally breached the citadel of eastern Christianity and now the scenes of 1204 were repeated. Men, women, and children were massacred without discrimination or pity. After the first orgy of slaughter the victorious Muslims systematically plundered churches, monasteries, palaces and houses. Great numbers of prisoners were taken and enslaved, and the booty which the Ottoman soldiery gathered was such as they had never seen before. The historian Ducas describes the plunder of the city in detail:

> Three days after the fall of the city he [Muhammed] released the ships so that each might sail off to its own province and city, each carrying such a load that it seemed each would sink. And what sort of a cargo? Luxurious cloths and textiles, objects and vessels of gold, silver, bronze, and brass, books beyond all counting and number, prisoners including priests and lay persons, nuns and monks. All the ships were full of cargoes, and the tents of the army camps were full of captives and of the above enumerated items and goods. And there was to be seen among the barbarian host one wearing the sakkon of an

190

archbishop, another wearing the gold epitrahelion of a priest, leading their dogs clothed instead of with the usual collars with gold brocaded amnous (ecclesiastical vestments). Others were to be seen seated at banquets, with the holy discs before them containing fruit and other foods, which they were eating, and with the holy chalices from which they drank their wine. And having loaded all the books, reaching unto a number beyond numbering, upon carts, they scattered them throughout the east and west. For one nomisma ten books could be bought (and what kind of books), Aristotelian, Platonic, theological, and every other kind. There were gospels which had every type of embellishment, beyond number, they smashed the gold and silver from them and some they sold, others they threw away. And all the icons were thrown into the flame, from which flame they broiled their meat.

After three days of horrible pillaging Muhammed entered Hagia Sophia, mounted the pulpit accompanied by an imam, and the Friday prayer was recited. The Sultan then entered the Christian sanctuary where he personally destroyed the altar, an act which symbolized the end of a thousand years of history.

Pitiful as was its end, the history of Byzantium nevertheless reads like a great epic. The Byzantines carried the torch of civilization unextinguished at a time when the barbarous Germanic and Slav tribes had reduced much of Europe to near chaos: and they maintained this high degree of civilization until western Europe gradually emerged and began to take form. It is no exaggeration to credit the empire with the preservation of European civilization from Islam in the seventh and eighth centuries. Had the empire fallen before the Arab attacks, Islam would have spread to much of Europe, with unforseeable consequences, while it was still in an amorphous state. The Slavonic east would doubtless have received the Islamic faith, as would much of central Europe. Italy, isolated between Muslim Spain and an Islam established in the Balkans and central Europe, would have been seriously threatened, and so would the papacy. Indeed, invasions from Arab-held Sicily might well have established the sway of Islam in the Italian peninsula.

The empire developed a great and original art which was decisive in much of the Slav world, and the influence of which is to be discerned in Venetian and Ottoman architecture as well as in some of the earlier schools of painting in Italy. Its civilization played an important rôle in the evolution of such widely divergent phenomena as religious music, monasticism and humanism in the west. Certainly one of its greatest services was the preservation of so much of the classical Greek literary heritage, an inheritance which is at the very basis of western humanism. And finally, it created Christian theology, the most impressive intellectual monument of the Middle Ages.

What is the relationship of Byzantium and the 'modern Byzantine derivatives' – that is, the Balkans and Russia – to Europe? Geographically, of course, these 'Byzantine derivatives' are part of

Europe. But historically speaking the answer is not so simple, for eastern and western Europe present strong differences, differences which were already visible by the time of Liudprand's embassy to the court of Nicephorus Phocas. The historical European civilization of which one usually speaks is that of the Latin-German west which, arising from the feudal age, developed and experienced the Renaissance, the Reformation, the Enlightenment and modern industrialism.

The Byzantine cultural area (especially Byzantium and the Balkans) began to feel the pressure of the west in the later Middle Ages and to undergo many of its influences in commercial life, military forms, technology, literature and art. But the military victories of the Altaic peoples (the Mongols in Russia, and the Turks in the Balkans) halted this development by re-orienting these societies toward the Muslim east. Consequently the encounter between Byzantium and the Latin west, which had begun so disastrously for the east but which seemed so promising, was postponed for four hundred years (until the nineteenth century), at which time the Balkan peoples were faced with the impossible task of bridging the gap between the Renaissance and the Industrial Revolution in a very brief space of time. In Russia, where the Mongol yoke was removed much earlier, the Tsars began to make the *rapprochement* with the west much earlier.

But if Byzantium differed from the west and had much that to western eyes smacked of the exotic Orient, Byzantine society was as different and distinct from Islamic as it was from western society. This is still evident to the traveller today who leaves central Europe and passes through the Balkans to the Islamic countries, for as the traveller moves eastward the degree of 'strangeness' increases. The Balkans form the transitional area between Europe and the Islamic Near East, and so it was in the Middle Ages. The west, Byzantium, and Islam developed in areas which in part had belonged to the Roman empire and therefore all three societies shared in the Graeco-Roman tradition. It is this fact which gives a vague unity to these three societies of the medieval period, in contrast to the societies of China, India and the Altai.

194

129 A group of Constaninople nuns, from a manuscript produced in that city about 1400 ▶

In the west this tradition was altered by the disappearance of the Greek element and the admixture of the Germanic strain, whereas in the Near East the Greek element had been weak. Though the early Arab conquerors were affected by their Byzantine environment and inherited much of Greek literary culture and Byzantine institutions, it was Persia and Arabia which finally predominated. Thus as the west and Islam gradually developed in their own ways, they moved further away from Byzantine civilization. Byzantium remained closest to the parent culture and though this endowed its society with great sophistication it also constituted shackles which deterred a more vigorous development. Byzantium represents a society and culture midway between those of Islam and the Latin west, more akin to either than the west was to Islam or Islam to the west. It was a result of this medial position that the Orthodox peoples were psychologically prepared to accept westernization at least a century before the Muslims, and that they have felt less ill at ease than the Muslims about the problems which such an adjustment has demanded.

SELECTED BIBLIOGRAPHY

HISTORY

G. Ostrogorsky, *Geschichte des byzantinischen Staates*, 3rd ed. (Munich 1963)
           History of the Byzantine State (New Brunswick 1957)

A. A. Vasiliev, *History of the Byzantine Empire*, 2 vols (Madison 1952)

L. Bréhier, *Vie et mort de Byzance* (Paris 1947)

N. Baynes, *Byzantine Studies and Other Essays* (London 1955)

K. Hopf, *Geschichte Griechenlands vom Beginne des Mittelalters bis auf die neure Zeit* (Leipzig 1867–68)

A. H. M. Jones, *The Later Roman Empire, 284–602: A Social, Economic, and Administrative Survey*, 3 vols (Oxford 1964)

J. B. Bury, *History of the Later Roman Empire from the Death of Theodosius I to the Death of Justinian (395–565)*, 2 vols (London 1923)

J. Fallmerayer, *Geschichte der Halbinsel Morea während des Mittelalters*, 2 vols (Stuttgart and Tübingen 1830–36)

E. Stein, *Histoire du bas empire*, 2 vols (Paris 1949, 1959)

N. Baynes, 'Constantine the Great and the Christian Church' in *Proceedings of the British Academy*, xv (1929), 341–442

H. Grégoire, 'Les Persecutions dans l'Empire romain' in *Mémoires de l'academie royale de Belgique. Classe des lettres et des sciences morales et politiques*, v. 46, pt. 1 (Brussels 1951)

A. H. M. Jones, *Constantine and the Conversion of Europe* (New York 1962)

A. Piganiol, *L'Empire chrétien, 325–95* (Paris 1947)

J. Bidez, *La vie de l'empereur Julien* (Paris 1930)

A. A. Vasiliev, *Justin the First. An Introduction to the Epoch of Justinian the Great* (Cambridge 1950)

A. Pernice, *L'Imperatore Eraclio, saggio di storia bizantina* (Florence 1905)

J. B. Bury, *A History of the Eastern Roman Empire from the Fall of Irene to the Accession of Basil I, 802–67* (London 1912)

A. Vogt, *Basile I, empereur de Byzance et la civilisation byzantine à la fin du IXᵉ siècle* (Paris 1908)

S. Runciman, *The Emperor Romanus Lecapenus and his Reign* (Cambridge 1929)

A. Rambaud, *L'Empire grec au Xᵉ siècle: Constantin Porphyrogénète* (Paris 1870)

G. Schlumberger, *Un Empereur byzantin au Xᵉ siècle: Nicéphore Phocas* (Paris 1890)
           L'Épopée byzantine à la fin du Xᵉ siècle, 3 vols (Paris 1896, 1900, 1905)

C. Neumann, 'La situation mondiale de l'empire byzantin avant les Croisades' in *Revue de l'orient latin*, x (1905), 57–171

R. J. H. Jenkins, *The Byzantine Empire on the Eve of the Crusades* (London 1953)

S. Vryonis, 'Byzantium: The Social Basis of Decline in the Eleventh Century' in *Greek, Roman and Byzantine Studies*, II (1959), 159–75

F. Chalandon, *Essai sur le règne d'Alexius I Comnène, 1081–1118* (Paris 1900)
Jean II Comnène (1118–1143) et Manuel I Comnène (1143–1180) (Paris 1912)

A. Meliarakes, *Istoria tou vasileiou tes Nikaias kai tou despotatou tes Epeirou, 1204–1261* (Athens 1898)

A. Gardner, *The Lascarids of Nicaea* (London 1912)

W. Miller, *Trebizond, the Last Greek Empire* (London 1926)

C. Diehl, 'L'Empire byzantin sous les Paléologues' in *Études byzantines* (Paris 1905)

D. Geanakoplos, *Emperor Michael Palaeologus and the West* (Cambridge 1959)

D. Zakynthinos, *Le despotat grec de Morée*, 2 vols (Paris 1932, Athens 1953)

P. Charanis, 'The Strife among the Palaeologoi and the Ottoman Turks, 1370–1402' in *Byzantion*, XVI (1942–43), 286–315

O. Halecki, *Un empereur de Byzance à Rome* (Warsaw 1930)

S. Runciman, *The Fall of Constantinople, 1453* (Cambridge 1965)

FOREIGN PEOPLES

J. Starr, *The Jews in the Byzantine Empire, 641–1204* (Athens 1939)

R. Grousset, *Histoire de l'Arménie des origines à 1071* (Paris 1947)

Fr. Tournebize, *Histoire politique et religieuse de l'Arménie depuis les origines des Arméniens jusqu'à la mort de leur dernier roi (l'an 1393)* (Paris 1900)

A. Christensen, *L'Iran sous les Sassanides*, 2nd ed. (Copenhagen 1944)

G. von Grunebaum, *Medieval Islam: A Study in Cultural Orientation*, 2nd ed. (Chicago 1953)

A. A. Vasiliev, *Byzance et les Arabes*, French ed. by H. Grégoire and M. Canard, 2 vols (Brussels 1935, 1950)

M. Canard, 'Les expeditions des Arabes contre Constantinople dans l'histoire et dans la légende' in *Journal asiatique*, XXVIII (1926), 61–121

G. Moravcsik, *Byzantinoturcica*, 2nd ed., 2 vols (Berlin 1958)

J. Laurent, *Byzance et les Turcs seljoucides dans l'Asie occidentale jusqu'en 1081* (Nancy 1913)

H. A. Gibbons, *The Foundation of the Ottoman Empire* (London 1916)

G. Arnakis, *Oi protoi Othomanoi* (Athens 1947)

F. Babinger, *Mahomet II, le Conquérant, et son temps, 1423–1481* (Paris 1954)

F. Dvornik, *The Slavs. Their Early History and Civilization* (Boston 1956)

K. Jireček, *Geschichte der Serben*, 2 vols (Gotha 1918)

S. Runciman, *A History of the First Bulgarian Empire* (London 1930)

F. Dvornik, *Les Slaves, Byzance et Rome au IXe siècle* (Paris 1926)

R. L. Wolff, 'The Second Bulgarian Empire: Its Origins and History to 1204' in *Speculum* XXIV (1949), 167–206

C. Diehl, *Une république patricienne. Venise* (Paris 1915)

H. F. Brown, 'The Venetians and the Venetian Quarter in Constantinople to the Close of the Twelfth Century' in *The Journal of Hellenic Studies*, XL (1920), 68–88

J. Longnon, *L'Empire latin de Constantinople et la principauté de Morée* (Paris 1949)

R. L. Wolff, 'The Organization of the Latin Patriarchate of Constantinople, 1204–1261. Social and Administrative Consequences of the Latin Conquest' in *Traditio*, VI (1948), 33–60

F. Chalandon, *Histoire de la domination normande en Sicile*, 2 vols (Paris 1907)

S. Runciman, *A History of the Crusades*, 3 vols (Cambridge 1951, 1952, 1954)

K. Setton, ed., *A History of the Crusades*, 2 vols (Philadelphia 1955, 1962)

W. Miller, *The Latins in the Levant: A History of Frankish Greece (1204–1566)* (London 1908)

K. M. Setton, *Catalan Domination of Athens, 1311–1388* (Cambridge 1948)

CHURCH AND RELIGION

F. Cumont, *Oriental Religions in Roman Paganism* (New York 1956)

H. G. Beck, *Kirche und theologische Literatur im byzantinischen Reich* (Munich 1959)

R. M. French, *The Eastern Orthodox Church* (London 1951)

T. Ware, *The Orthodox Church* (Suffolk 1964)

M. Anastos, 'Nestorius was Orthodox' in *Dumbarton Oaks Papers*, No. 16 (1962), 119–40

P. Charanis, *Church and State in the Later Roman Empire. The Religious Policy of Anastasius the First, 419–518* (Madison 1939)

E. J. Martin, *A History of the Iconoclastic Controversy* (London 1930)

F. Dvornik, *The Photian Schism, History and Legend* (Cambridge 1948)

L. Bréhier, *Le schisme oriental du XIe siècle* (Paris 1899)

S. Runciman, *The Eastern Schism. A Study of the Papacy and the Eastern Churches during the XIth and XIIth Centuries* (Oxford 1955)

W. Norden, *Das Papsttum und Byzanz* (Berlin 1903, reprinted 1965)

SOCIETY

L. Bréhier, *Les institutions de l'empire byzantin* (Paris 1949)
                La civilisation byzantine (Paris 1950)

Ph. Koukoules, *Vizantinon vios kai politismos*, 5 vols (Athens 1948–52)

G. Downey, *A History of Antioch in Syria: From Seleucus to the Arab Conquest* (Princeton 1961)

M. Manojlovič, 'Le peuple de Constantinople de 400 à 800 après J. C. Étude spéciale de ses forces armées, des éléments qui le composaient et de son rôle constitutionnel pendant cette période' in *Byzantion*, XI (1936), 617–716

E. E. Lipšic, *Očerki istorii vizantijskogo obščestva i kul'tury, VIII–pervaja polovine IX veka* (Moscow-Leningrad 1961)

A. P. Každan, *Derevnja i gorod v Vizantii IX-X vv.* (Moscow 1960)

S. Vryonis, 'Byzantine Demokratia and the Guilds in the Eleventh Century' in *Dumbarton Oaks Papers*, No. 17 (1963), 289–314

P. Charanis, 'The Monastic Properties and the State in the Byzantine Empire' in *Dumbarton Oaks Papers*, No. 4 (1948), 51–118

G. Ostrogorsky, 'Agrarian Conditions in the Byzantine Empire in the Middle Ages' in *Cambridge Economic History*, 1 (Cambridge 1941), 194–223

R. Janin, *Constantinople byzantine, Développement urbain et répertoire topographique* (Paris 1950)

A. Stöckle, *Spätrömische und byzantinische Zünfte* (Leipzig 1911)

F. Dölger, *Byzanz und die europäische Staatenwelt* (Ettal 1953)

O. Treitinger, *Die oströmische Kaiser- und Reichsidee nach ihrer Gestaltung im höfischen Zeremoniell* (Jena 1938)

C. Diehl, *La société byzantine à l'époque des Comnènes* (Paris 1929)

M. Anastos, 'The Ancient Greek Sources of Byzantine Absolutism' in *Harry Austryn Wolfson Jubilee Volume* (Jerusalem 1965), 89–109

ART, LITERATURE AND LEARNING

C. Diehl, *Manuel d'art byzantin*, 2nd ed., 2 vols (Paris 1925–26)

O. M. Dalton, *Byzantine Art and Archaeology* (Oxford 1911)

D. T. Rice, *The Art of Byzantium* (London 1959)
    Art of the Byzantine Era (London 1963)

A. Grabar, *The Great Centuries of Byzantine Painting* (Geneva 1953)

V. N. Lazarev, *Istoria vizantiiskoi zhivopisi*, 2 vols (Moscow, 1947–48)

A. Grabar, *L'Empereur dans l'art byzantin* (Paris 1936)

E. Kitzinger, 'The Cult of Images in the Age before Iconoclasm' in *Dumbarton Oaks Papers*, No. 8 (1954), 83–150

K. Weitzmann, *Geistige Grundlagen und Wesen der makedonischen Renaissance* (Cologne and Opladen 1963)
    Die byzantinische Buchmalerei des IX und X Jahrhunderts (Berlin 1935)

E. Diez and O. Demus, *Byzantine Mosaics in Greece* (Cambridge 1931)

A. Xyngopoulos, *Thessalonique et la peinture macédonienne* (Athens 1955)

K. Krumbacher, *Geschichte der byzantinischen Literatur von Justinian bis zum Ende des oströmischen Reiches (527–1453)*, 2nd ed. (Munich 1897)

F. Fuchs, *Die höheren Schulen von Konstantinopel im Mittelalter* (Leipzig and Berlin 1926)

J. Mavrogordato, *Digenes Akrites* (Oxford 1956)

K. M. Setton, 'The Byzantine Background to the Italian Renaissance' in *Proceedings of the American Philosophical Society*, C (1956), 1–76

H-G. Beck, *Theodore Metochites. Die Krise der byzantinischen Weltbildes im 14 Jahrhundert* (Munich 1952)

D. Geanakoplos, *Greek Scholars in Venice* (Cambridge 1962)

K. E. Zacharia von Lingenthal, *Geschichte des griechisch-römischen Rechts*, 3rd ed. (Berlin 1892)

E. Wellesz, *A History of Byzantine Music and Hymnography*, 2nd ed. (Oxford 1961)

LIST OF ILLUSTRATIONS

28 The Golden Gate and walls of Constantinople from the south. c. 400. Photo: Hirmer

29 Hagia Eirene, Constantinople. Exterior. c. 532 and later. Photo: Hirmer

30 Yeribatan-Saray. Underground cisterns built by Justinian. Photo: Hirmer

31 The Aqueduct of Valens, Constantinople. Built 368. Photo: Hirmer

32 Hagia Sophia, Constantinople. Interior. Built 532–7. Engraving after Fossati: *Aya Sophia, Constantinople, as recently restored by order of H.M. the Sultan Abdul Medjiel.* London, 1852

33 'Rubens vase'. Agate. c. 400 A D. Walters Art Gallery, Baltimore

34 The Personification of India. Silver dish. Sixth century. Archaeological Museum, Constantinople. Photo: Hirmer

35 Cross of Justin II. Silver gilt. c. 575. Capella delle Reliquie, Basilica Vaticana, Rome. Photo: Mansell-Alinari

36 Throne of Archbishop Maximian. John the Baptist and the four Evangelists. Ivory. Sixth century. Museo dell' Arcivescovado, Ravenna. Photo: Hirmer

37 *Multi-solidus* gold piece of Justinian. 534–8. Electrotype of gold original formerly in the Cabinet des Médailles, Paris. British Museum, London. Photo: Peter Clayton

38 Gold *solidus* of Phocas. Probably issued 603. P. D. Whitting Collection. Photo: Peter Clayton

39 Gold *solidus* of Heraclius and Constantine. 613–29. P. D. Whitting Collection. Photo: Peter Clayton

40 Gold *solidus* of Heraclius and Constantine. 629–31. P. D. Whitting Collection. Photo: Peter Clayton

41 Statue of Heraclius. Bronze. 610–41. Barletta. Photo: Hirmer.

42 Reverse type of a bronze coin of Abd al Malik. P. D. Whitting Collection. Photo: Peter Clayton

43 Mecca. Engraving by Hunglinger showing the Ka'ba. 1803. British Museum, London. Photo: R. B. Fleming & Co. Ltd

44 Gold *solidus* of Constantine V (obverse). 741–75. P. D. Whitting Collection. Photo: Peter Clayton

45 Gold *solidus* with portrait of the Empress Irene. 797–802. British Museum, London. Photo: John Webb

46 The wars of Nicephorus I against Krum and the capture of Nicephorus. Illuminations from Slavonic copy of the Manasses Codex. 1345. Vatican Library, Rome

47 Gold *solidus* of Justinian II, the reverse showing Christ, King of Kings. 685–95. P. D. Whitting Collection. Photo: Peter Clayton

48 Gold *solidus* of Leo III. 717–41. P. D. Whitting Collection. Photo: Peter Clayton

49 Iconoclast whitewashing an image. Miniature from the Chludov Psalter. Ninth century. Public Library, Moscow. Photo: Collection de l'Ecole des Hautes Etudes, Paris

50 Mosaic cross in the apse of Hagia Eirene, Constantinople. Eighth to ninth centuries. Photo: Courtesy of the Byzantine Institute Inc.

51 Theodora restores the icons. Ms. Gr. 1613. fol. 392. Vatican Library, Rome

52 The Adoration and the Nativity. Ivory diptych. Sixth century. British Museum, London. Photo: Hirmer

53 The Nativity. Manuscript with Syriac text. 1216–20. British Museum, London. Photo: Courtesy of the Trustees of the British Museum

54 The Great Mosque of Damascus. Architectural scene from above the entrance of the courtyard. Mosaic. 715. Photo: J. E. Dayton

55 SS. Cyril and Methodius kneeling before Christ. Fresco in San Clemente, Rome. Eleventh century. From J. Wilpert—*Die Römischen Mosaiken und Malereien*

56 Leo VI receiving the investiture of Holy Wisdom. Detail of mosaic. Hagia Sophia, Constantinople. Late ninth century. Photo: Thames and Hudson archives

57 Weight representing Nicephorus Phocas, died A D 610. British Museum. Photo: Courtesy of the Trustees of the British Museum

58 Gold *solidus*. John I Tzimisces crowned by the Virgin. P. D. Whitting Collection. Photo: Peter Clayton

59 Epiphany of the Emperor Constantine VII Porphyrogenitus. Ivory relief. *c.* 944. Museum of Fine Art, Moscow. Photo: Hirmer

60 Portrait of the Emperor Basil II Bulgaroctonos. From the Psalter of Basil II. 976–1025 (Cod. Gr. 17) Biblioteca Marciana, Venice. Photo: Hirmer

61 Work in the vineyards. Miniature from a copy of the Gospels. Eleventh century. Bibliothèque Nationale, Paris

62 Sheep-shearing, sailing, ploughing. Miniatures from a copy of the Sermons of St Gregory of Nazianzus. Eleventh century. Bibliothèque Nationale, Paris

63 Silenus and a dancing Maenad. Silver and silver-gilt dish. 610–29. State Hermitage Museum, Leningrad. Photo: S. C. R. Library

64 Chalice bearing the name of the Emperor Romanus. Gold, precious stones and cloisonné enamel. *c.* 1070. Treasury of St Mark's, Venice. Photo: Osvaldo Böhm

65 The Harbaville Triptych. Centre panel. Ivory. Late tenth century. Louvre, Paris. Photo: Hirmer

66 Two riders hunting lions. Fragment of silk textile. Mid-eighth century. Musée Historique des Tissus, Lyon. Photo: Giraudon

67 Pattern of eagles. Detail from the Shroud of St Germain l'Auxerrois. Silk. Late tenth century. Church of St Eusebius, Auxerre. Photo: Giraudon

68 A lion strangler. Silk textile. Eighth century. Victoria and Albert Museum, London. Photo: Hirmer

69 St Luke. From an eleventh-century Gospel. Add. Ms. 28815. fol. 76v. British Museum, London. Photo: Courtesy of the Trustees of the British Museum

70 The Monastery of St Catherine, Mount Sinai. Photo: Beno Rothenberg

71 The Virgin and Child with saints and eagles. Icon on the church of St Catherine, Mount Sinai. Sixth century. Photo: Institut Français d'Athène

72 Tokale Kilise, Cappadocia. Wall-painting, showing earlier and later layers. Photo: Josephine Powell

73 The church of St John of Studium, Constantinople. Interior, looking east. *c.* 463. Photo: Hirmer

74 Christ Pantocrator. Mosaic. *c.* 1100. The dome, Daphni, Greece. Photo: David Talbot Rice

75 Illumination from the *Theriaca* of Nicandor. Tenth century. Suppl. Gr. 247 f. 47v. Bibliothèque Nationale, Paris

76 The Rape of Europa. Detail of lid of the Veroli Casket. Ivory. Tenth century to eleventh century. Victoria and Albert Museum, London

77 Reliquary for the True Cross. Enamels at centre of the outer container. *c.* 955. Cathedral Treasury, Limburg on the Lahn. Photo: Hirmer

78 Constantine, Zoe, Theodora. Enamel plaques from the crown of Constantine Monomachos. 1042–55. National Museum, Budapest. Photo: Hirmer

79 David composing the Psalms. From the Paris Psalter. Ninth century. Ms. Gr. 139. Bibliothèque Nationale, Paris. Photo: Hirmer

80 Paradise and the Four Rivers. From the Homilies of Jacob of Kokinobaphos. Twelfth century. Ms. Gr. 1208. Bibliothèque Nationale, Paris

81 The Crowning of Romanus II and Eudoxia. Ivory. *c.* 950. Cabinet des Médailles, Paris. Photo: Hirmer

82 The Emperor Nicephorus Botaniates, St John Chrysostom and an angel. Miniature from the Homilies of St John Chrysostom. *c.* 1078. ms. Coislin 79. f. 2v. Bibliothèque Nationale, Paris. Photo: Hirmer

83 Gold *solidus* of Isaac I Comnenus. 969–76. P. D. Whitting Collection. Photo: Peter Clayton

84 Holy Crown of Hungary. Gold and enamel. 1074–7. Budapest Treasury. Photo: Marburg

115 Andrew Palaeologus. Fresco by Bernardino Pinturicchio. Appartamente Borgia, Vatican, Rome. Photo: Mansell-Alinari

116 John VIII Palaeologus. Fresco by Benozzo Gozzoli. Medici Palace, Florence. Photo: Mansell-Alinari

117 The town of Mistra. Mostly fourteenth century. Photo: Josephine Powell

118 The Entry into Jerusalem. Detail of wall-painting. *c.* 1380. Church of the Peribleptos, Mistra. Photo: Josephine Powell

119 Theodore Metochites. Detail of mosaic. 1320–30. Tympanum of Kariye Jami, Constantinople. Photo: Byzantine Institute, Washington

120 Christ Pantocrator. Mosaic. 1300–20. Kariye Jami, Constantinople. Photo: Hirmer

121 Portrait of Hippocrates. From a manuscript of Hippocrates. *c.* 1342. Ms. Gr. 2144, f. 10. Bibliothèque Nationale, Paris. Photo: Hirmer

122 Two Shepherds. Detail from The Nativity. *c.* 1312. Church of the Holy Apostles, Salonica. After Xyngopoulos, *Thessalonique et la Peinture Macedonienne*, Athens, 1955

123 Church of the Holy Apostles, Salonica. East end. *c.* 1312. Photo: Collection de l'Ecole des Hautes Etudes, Paris

124 Hagia Maria Pammarkaristos, Fetiye Jami, Constantinople. East end. Thirteenth century. Photo: Martin Hürlimann

125 The Anastasis. Wall-painting. *c.* 1310. Kariye Jami (Church of St Saviour), Constantinople. Photo: Byzantine Institute, Washington

126 Rumeli Hisar. Fort built on the Bosphorus by Muhammed II. Photo: Martin Hürlimann

127 Portrait of Sultan Muhammed II. Gentile Bellini. 1480. National Gallery, London

128 The Siege of Constantinople. 1453. From Bertrandon de la Broquière: *Voyage d'outremer*, 1455. Bibliothèque Nationale, Paris. Ms. Fr. 9087, v. 207

129 Group of Nuns. From the Lincoln College, Typicon. *c.* 1400. Ms. Gr. 35, f. 12r. Bodleian Library, Oxford

The maps were drawn by Mrs P. S. Verity

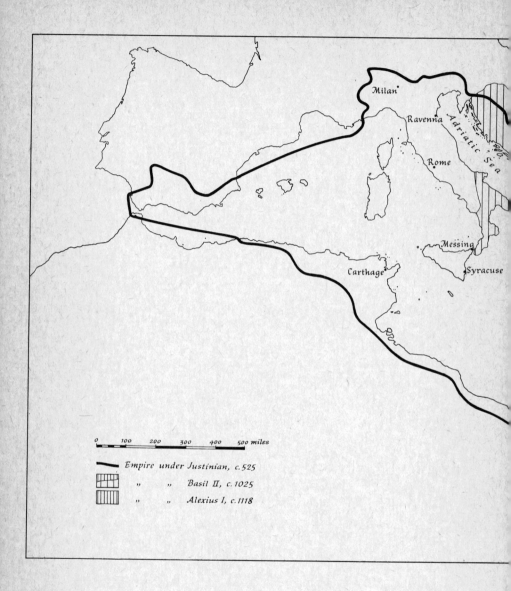

Milan

Ravenna

Rome

Adriatic Sea

Messina

Carthage

Syracuse

0   100   200   300   400   500 miles

━━━ Empire under Justinian, c. 525

▦   „   „   Basil II, c. 1025

▥   „   „   Alexius I, c. 1118

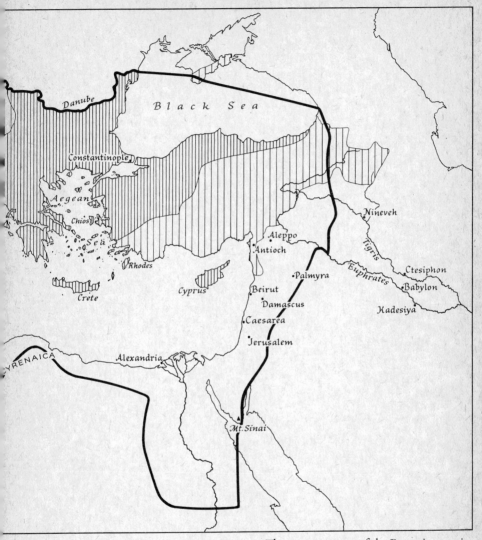

The greatest extent of the Byzantine empire

The core of the Byzantine empire

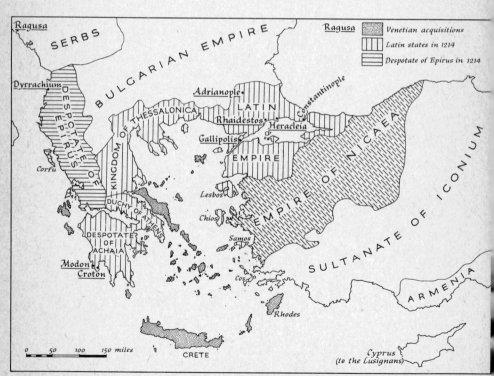

The Latin states after the fall of Constantinople in 1203

INDEX

213

Nicander, 118
Nicephorus I, 71, *46*
Nicephorus II Phocas, 86–92, 106, 112, 194, *57*
Nicephorus III Botaniates, *82*
Nicetas, 114
Nicholas V, Pope, 187
Nicomedia, 26, 158, 174
Nicopolis, 176
Normans, 124, 131, 134, 136, 139, 141, 145, 149, *89*
Notaras, Lucas, 187

Ochrid, 148, 165
Odenathus of Palmyra, 15–16
Odovacer, 34
Oppian, 118
Orhan, 174
Origen, 41
Orthodox Church, 60, 83, 99, 101–8, 130, 139, 161, 177, 196
Osman, 174
Ostrogoths, 30, 34, 46, 68
Otto I, 91
Otto de la Roche, 160
Ottomans, 132, 169, 174–7, 181, 187–93, *113*

Palaeologoi, 168, 178–9. *See also* Emperors of Byzantium, 8
Palaeologus, Andrew, *115*
Palamas, Gregory, 170
Palestine, 38, 58, 62–4, 103, 145, 150, 174
Parthia, 14
Patmos, 108
Patras, 82, 98
Patzinaks, 30, 124, 130–1, 133, 136, 138, 141, *89*

Paulicians, 84–6
Pelagonia, 165
Peloponnese, *see* Morea
Pepin, 66
Pergamum, 158
Perinthus, 30
Persia, 19–20, 22; Persians, 58–60, 62–3
Peter III of Aragon, 167
Peter of Bulgaria, 90
Philip of Swabia, 150–1
Philippopolis, 86
Phocas (Emperor), 58, 69, *38, 41*
Phocas family, 84, 126
Phocas, Bardas, 91–2, 99, 127
Photius, 84, 138
Pisa, 144, 145
Planudes, Maximus, 181
Pletho, 178, 181–2
Procopius, 42
Prusa, 104, 158, 174–5
Psellus, Michael, 112, 115–16, 121, 123–6, 132, 148
Ptochoprodromus, Theodore, 149

Ragusa, 160
Ravenna, 66, 71, *15, 23, 24, 25*
Rhodes, 63
Romanus I Lecapenus, 85–6, 90, 112, 127
Romanus II, *81*
Romanus IV Diogenes, 130, 132–3
Romanus Melodus, 52
Rome, 26–7, 32, 37, 39, 46, 66, 138
Rumeli Hisar, 187, *126*
Russia, 30, 99, 121, 131, 146, *98*

St Anthony, 112
St Athanasius, 104, 106